AF539772

HUMAN RESOURCE MANAGEMENT

By
Dr. M. Lakshmi Narasaiah,
M.A., Ph.D.,
Professor and Head,
Department of Economics,
Sri Krishnadevaraya University Post-graduate Centre,
Kurnool–518002
A.P. (India)

2003

DISCOVERY PUBLISHING HOUSE
NEW DELHI-110002

First Published-2003
Reprint : 2012
ISBN 81-7141-669-1

Published by
DISCOVERY PUBLISHING HOUSE
4831/24, Ansari Road, Prahlad Street,
Darya Ganj, New Delhi-110002 (India)
Phone: 3279245 • Fax: 91-11-3253475
E-mail:dphtemp@indiatimes.com

Printed at: Dynamic Printers

PREFACE

In contrast to the food supply challenge posed by the coming wave of population growth, the global need for teachers and classrooms will rise very slowly in the next half-century. In many countries, the school-age population is increasing much less rapidly than the overall national population. The trend illustrates that growth rates typically differ for different age strata of the population. It also shows that declining birth rates can take decades to move through an entire population.

At the global level, for example, total population is projected to increase by 54 per cent between 2000 and 2050, but the number of children aged 5 to 14 will grow by only 6 per cent. And of the world's largest countries—accounting for 60 per cent of global population in 1995—will actually begin to see decreases in the number of children aged 5 to 14 by 2015; for several of these countries, the decline in this age group has already begun. These countries will need fewer classrooms and teachers to educate the youngest members of society (assuming they maintain current class size and student-teacher ratios).

Plenty of nations, however, still have increasing child-age populations. Where countries have not acted to stabilize population, the base of the national population pyramid continues to expand, and pressures on the educational system will be severe. In the world's 10 fastest-growing countries, for example, most of which are in Africa and the Middle East, the child-age population will increase in average 93 per cent over the next half-century. Africa as a whole will see its school-age population grow by 75 per cent through 2040.

The rapid growth in African populations is especially worrisome because of the extra burden it imposes in a region already lagging in education. Only 56 per cent of Africans south of the Sahara are literate, compared with 71 per cent for all developing countries. Few African countries have universal primary education, and secondary education reaches only 4-5 per cent of African children. Educating today's children is challenge enough; the addition of another three students for every four already there will require heroic investments in education. But the alternative is grim: without additional investments in education, today's average student-teacher ratio of 42 in sub-Saharan Africa will reach 75 by 2040.

Many countries will be challenged to increase funding for education while ensuring that other worthy sectors also receive the support they need. With 900 million illiterate adults in the world, the case for a renewed commitment to education is easy to make. But competiting for these funds are the 840 million chronically hungry and the 1.2 billion without access to a decent toilet.

Contents

Preface

1. Will Education Go To Market? 1
2. Private Education: The Poor's Best Chance? 6
3. Corporate Ambitions in Education 11
4. Violence in Schools: A World-wide Affair 15
5. Helping Your Child Learn 17
6. Promotion of Higher Education in Research 19
7. Wanted: A New Deal for the Universities 23
8. Shaking the Ivory Tower 29
9. Wiring Up the Ivory Towers 37
10. Management Training in India 42
11. For a Broader Approach to Education 47
12. Policy Researchers and Policy Makers: Never the Twain Shall Meet? 51
13. Population Growth and Education 56
14. No Progress Without A Secular Society 59

15. Solving the Unemployment Problem by Looking Beyond the Job 62

16. Towards Healthy Cities 66

17. Children's Health and the Environment 71

18. The Environment, the Economy and Public Health—An Integrated View 74

19. Action for Safe Motherhood 79

20. Safe Motherhood is a Human Rights Issue 83

21. What is Known About Reducing Maternal Mortality? 86

22. Why don't We Stop Tuberculosis 88

23. AIDS and the Responsibility of the Media 91

24. Controlling the Global Tobacco Epidemic Towards a Transnational Response 95

25. Taking Poverty to Heart: Non-Communicable Diseases and the Poor 98

26. Health Care Relief in Conflict Situations 102

27. Stop Child Labour 109

28. World Trade—The Next Challenge 116

29. Rural Poverty in India 121

30. Technological Entrepreneurship: The New Force for Economic Growth 127

Bibliography 133

Index 143

1

Will Education Go To Market?

The World Trade Organisation has launched processes that could open up to competition the expanding and highly protected world market in education. What issues are at stake? Most of us see education as first and foremost a public service which is responsible for providing young people with instruction. For investors looking for somewhere to put their money it is also an annual budget of $1,000 billion worldwide, a sector employing 50 million people, and above all a billion potential customers in the form of students.

The decision to extend to services the liberalisation of international trade which previously applied to commodities was taken in 1994. The General Agreement on Trade in Services (GATS) which was signed in April of that year included education on the list of services to be liberalised. To say outside the scope of this agreement a country's education system must be completely financed and administered by the state, which is no longer the case anywhere. However, each country can still decide freely what commitments it wants to make, and especially which educational sectors it wants to expose to market forces. The

New Zealand government, for example, has decided to open up to outside competition the whole private education sector, from primary to university level.

So far, New Zealand is an exception, but that situation is likely to change. Part 4 of the GATS agreement ('Progressive liberalisation) requires that fresh negotiations should be held by the end of 2000 at the latest, and should be directed to "the elimination of the adverse effects on trade in services of measures as a means of providing effective market access". At the Geneva headquarters of the World Trade Organisation (WTO), far from the headlines and the demonstrators, work still goes on. But independently of the WTO and national policies, a number of factors are driving educational systems towards 'communication'.

Pressures for Change

First, education is a rapidly-growing sector in which governments are finding it harder and harder to satisfy demand, above all in higher education. Between 1985 and 1992, the number of students in higher education rose about 26 per cent—from 58.6 to 73.7 million. Meanwhile, public spending on education has tended to stagnate over the past 15 years (5-6 per cent of GDP in rich countries and 4 per cent elsewhere).

In view of this dearth of public spending, parents and students are increasingly looking to private education for a solution. In the United States, every episode of violence in a state school and every scandal that rocks official school systems gives a boost to 'home schooling', where children no longer attend school and are taught at home.

Traditional public education is also coming in for strong criticism. Employees complain it is not geared to their needs and is not flexible enough. Under pressure from economic interests, a process of 'deregulating' education systems has begun. The growing independence of schools is encouraging them to look for alternative sources of funding, ranging from sponsorship to full management by private companies and including many kinds of partnerships between schools and firms. The time for out-of-school education has come...the liberalisation of the educational process thereby made possible will lead to control by education service providers who are more innovative than the traditional structures.

The development and spread of information and communication technologies on a massive scale make possible the development of paid distance learning, using multimedia and the Internet for tutorials, examinations, etc.

Secondary and primary education are also affected. More and more paying Internet sites bill themselves as alternatives to state schools or traditional private schools. The computer screen takes over from the teacher for a free of around $2,250 a year.

The WTO secretariat set up a working group in 1998 to look at prospectus for more liberalised education. Its report pointed to the rapid growth of distance learning and noted the increasing number of partnerships between educational institutions and private firms.

Education for Export

Some 350 U.S. experts on international trade in services, including 170 businessmen and women, gathered at the U.S. Commerce Department in Washington on October 16, 1998 to draw up recommendations for the U.S. negotiators at the WTO. The purpose of the meeting, called Services 2000, was to look at how the U.S. government should continue to support the efforts of American business to take competitive advantage in foreign markets. The U.S. currently controls about 16 per cent of the world market in services. Its services exports have more than doubled in the past 10 years and now cover 42 per cent of the non-services trade deficit.

The United States is also the world's leading exporter of educational services, and a working group at the Services 2000 conference paid special attention to this sector. It concluded that the sector "needs the same degree of transparency, transferability and interchangeability, mutual recognition, and freedom from undue regulation or restraints and barriers that the United States acknowledges on behalf of other service industries". The report said that three points should be at the centre of WTO negotiations about education.

Firstly, there should be a free flow of electronic information and means of communication, nationally and internationally. Secondly, the negotiators should tackle "barriers and other restrictions that limit or prevent the provision of educational and training services across countries and internationally". They were also to deal with obstacles to the transferability of degrees and diplomas.

Fighting for Market Share

The U.S. demands are backed by most countries of the APEC (Asia-Pacific Economic Cooperation) zone. In a note in October 1999, the Australian delegation to the WTO said it would be "encouraging all members to make expanded commitments in all sectors, even the ones that have proved difficult in both regional and multilateral services negotiations", particularly education.

South Korea took a similar position. At a meeting of ministers of human resources from APEC Countries that it hosted in September 1997, the Seoul government put out a memorandum which clearly stated its vision of education as a tool of economic competition.

"The emphasis on education for itself or on education for good members of a community without a large emphasis on preparation for future work is no longer appropriate." Such a view of education and work cannot be justified in a world where economic development is emphasized.

"At present, in many economies, the education systems do not sufficiently reflect labour market conditions. Their inflexible and inefficient education systems could not meet the new economic environmental challenges". So education should be made more 'flexible', *i.e.* be deregulated and liberalised. In particular, "School systems should be established to allow all students to study what they are interested in" and "employers, with school educators, should share the role of educating students".

Some think resistance to liberalising education will come from Europe especially France. "The future WTO negotiations cannot call in question France's tradition of public service in the field of education and health," stressed a report on the WTO.

2

Private Education: The Poor's Best Chance?

Across the developing world, private schools and education companies are not only flourishing, but reaching the poor. India is a case in point. A common assumption about the private sector in education is that it caters only to the elite, and that its promotion only serves to exacerbate inequality. On the contrary recent research points in the opposite direction. If we want to help some of the most disadvantages groups in society, then encouraging deeper private sector involvements is likely to be the best way forward.

Several developments are underway in India, all of which involve the private education sector meeting the needs of the poor in distinct ways. But India is not unique in this respect—similar phenomena are happening all over the developing world.

As a point of departure, how do government schools serve the poor? Usefully, the government sponsored Public Report on Basic Education in India (PROBE) from 1999 paints a very bleak picture of the 'malfunctioning' of government schools for the poor. When researchers called unannounced on their random sample of schools, only 53 per cent had any 'teaching activity' going on. In 33 per cent, the head teacher was absent. Alarmingly, the team noted that the deterioration of teaching standards was not to do with disempowered teachers, but instead could be ascribed to 'plain negligence'. They noted "several cases of irresponsible teachers keeping a school closed... for months at a time, "many cases of drunk teachers, and head teachers who asked children to do domestic chores. Significantly, the low level of teaching activity occurred even in those schools with relative good infrastructure, teaching aids and pupil-teacher ratios.

But is there any alternative to these schools? Surely no-one else can do better than government given the resources available? As it happens, the PROBE report were serving the poor and conceded—rather reluctantly—such problems were not found in these schools. In the great majority of private schools—again visited unannounced and at random—"there was feverish classroom activity". Most parents would prefer to send their children to private schools if they could afford them. Private schools, they said, were successful because they were more accountable: "the teachers are accountable to the manager (who can fire them), and, through him or her, to the parents (who can withdraw their children)." Such accountability was not present in the government schools, and "this contrast is perceived with crystal clarity by the vast majority of parents".

The Way Forward: Loosen Regulations and Set Up Voucher Schemes

To many readers, the existence of these private schools for the poor will come as a surprise. It was to me too, until I had the privilege of conducting field work for the International Finance Corporation (the private finance arm of the World Bank) on a group of such schools operating under the banner of the Federation of Private Schools" management based in Hyderabad. The federation has 500 private schools (from kindergarten to grade ten) serving poor communities in slums and villages. I was impressed by both the entrepreneurial spirit within these schools—they were run on commercial principles, not dependent on hand-outs from state or philanthropy—but also be the spirit of dedication within the schools for the poor communities served: not for nothing were the leaders of the schools known as 'social workers' but these schools suffer under restrictive and inappropriate regulations. One example will suffice: to be recognised a school must deposit upto 50,000 rupees (about $1.200) in a stipulated bank account, of which neither the capital nor the interest can be touched. Given that the fees charged in these schools ranged from 25 (60 cents) to Rs. 150 per month (about $3.50) with most of the schools grouped near the lower end of the range, such sums are completely prohibitive.

Fees of around $ 10 per year are not affordable by everyone, but they are to a large number of poor families. Furthermore, the great majority of the schools offer a significant number of free places—up to 20 per cent—for the poorest students, allocated on the basis of claims of need checked informally in the community.

All of this suggests that if one is interested in serving the needs of the poor in India, then trying to reform the totally inadequate, cumbersome and unaccountable government system is unlikely to be the best way. Instead, reform the regulatory environment to make it suitable for the flourishing of private schools for the poor, help build private financing schemes using overseas and indigenous philanthropy, and encourage public voucher schemes so that parents can use their allowance of funding where they see the schools are performing well, rather than wasting them in unresponsive state schools.

Private education in developing countries isn't just about the poor, of course, and there are many exciting examples of big education businesses. But these too have implications for the ways in which the private sector can reach the least advantaged. One Indian company which embodies much of the excite the National Institute for Information Technology (NIIT). With its competitor, Aptech, it shares just over 70 per cent of the information technology education and training market in India estimated at roughly Rs. 1.1 billion ($ 24 million). NIIT has 40 wholly owned centres in the metropolitan areas, and about 1,000 franchised centres across India. It also has a global reach, with centres in the U.S. Asian Pacific, Europe, Japan, Central Asia and Africa. A key aspect of NIIT's educational philosophy is that there is a need to harness research to improve the efficiency of learning and to raise educational standards.

Because of its success in developing innovative and cost-effective IT education and training, NIIT has attracted the attention of several state governments. First off the mark was Tamil Nadu, which wanted to bring a computer curriculum to all of its high schools. Significantly, although allocating about $22 million over five years to this endeavour, it didn't hand the funds over to government schools, perhaps in light of the PROBE report's lessons. Instead, it developed a model to contract out the service to private companies, which provide the software and hardware, while the government supplies electricity and the class room. For the first round of the Tamil Nadu process, 43 contracts were awarded for 666 schools, with NIIT allotted 371 schools. Many of the classrooms have become NIIT centre, open to school children and teachers in daytime, then used by the franchise holder in the evenings. The contracting out of curriculum areas such as this represents an important step forward in relationships between the public and private sectors, and provides an interesting model worth watching and emulating.

Most recently, NIIT has focused on reaching largely illiterate and unschooled children through the Internet.

Within weeks of having set up an 'Internet kiosk' in a slum area, the institute's researchers found that without any instruction, children could achieve a remarkable level of computer literacy. NIIT is exploring ways to roll out the idea commercially, harnessing the power of the private sector to reach the poorest through modern technology.

These initiatives all find echoes in other developing countries. In each case, the private, not the public sector, is most responsive to the needs of the poor, and is bringing innovation, efficiency and educational quality to the lives of the most disadvantaged. The private sector has the potential to promote greater equity and to influence education policy, provided it is encouraged and viewed as a partner, not a threat to governments, whether in the developing or the developed world.

3

Corporate Ambitions in Education

Centralisation and efficiency, frequently invoking the powerful metaphor of scientific management or 'Taylorism', using the stopwatch and management to discover the 'one best way'. These principles had been instrumental, industrialists of the time believed, in creating the industrial revolution and the wealth of powerful international companies. The quest for efficiency of those decades led to the problems we must now repair, notably the rigid and bureaucratic structure of our school systems.

Today, public schools continue to adapt new business efficiency techniques in what seems to be a constant recycling process. Scientific management, it turns out, was only the precursor to a host of ever newer management theories aimed at encouraging greater worker productivity and hence greater national wealth.

When Schools Become Levers to Attract Business Investment

These trends have echoes in the management reforms prescribed for and adopted by schools. Some seek increased efficiency through decentralised school governance while others imagine that outsourcing (or contracting) the management and operation of schools will lift educators' performance because incentives are lacking in secure government jobs.

All this is happening against the backdrop of economic globalisation, which inevitably creates political tensions by pitting governments against one another in competition for transnational corporate jobs and global capital. Our current era mimics the turn of the century to the extent that international capital flows and transnational production processes influence both corporation and governments. Today, technologically induced speed, growth among investors, concentration of wealth, and interconnectedness have increased the effects of this global speculation and decreased the capacity of governments to regulate business and markets. Not surprisingly, this global market ideology has been broadly recognised as a force in national education policy.

Reforming local schools becomes one of the ways that cities engage in the global competition to provide production resources to corporations. When formal schooling is seen as a key element of productive capacity, a view reinforced by the decline of manufacturing and the rise of information-based technologies, the quality of the local public school system takes on renewed importance for business leaders and local politicians alike. Today's corporate leaders have uncommon access to elect political officials and government agency heads, the wealth of large corporations to draw upon, and the ability to affect local and regional economics simply by making business decisions.

Schools are treated as engines of economic development to lure business to a particular city or state, so corporate and local political leaders corporate in their governance and redesign. In short, school policy becomes labour policy?

This powerful combination of corporate, national and state executives is happening at the expenses of education professionals. In contrast to the turn of the century, when educators played a pivotal role in debates by emphasizing the role of schools in developing citizenship, today they have been largely discredited. Selecting school leaders from outside the field has become both symptom and spur to this decrease in the educator's status. A small but influential group of school districts is choosing leaders from among the ranks of businessmen, politicians and the military, rather than educators.

All this is taking place with little evidence that recent management solutions will turn around poor schools, nor that improvements in school performance protect against declines in productivity or the business cycle. Yet there are more troubling problems with reform strategies that pit the market against government in education. One is that education is reduced to its narrowest economic purposes. According to a 1992 survey, corporate executives most want schools to emphasize "a basic understanding of maths and science:" and "sound work habits such as self-discipline, timeliness and dedication to work." These are laudable goals, but reflect a narrow set of traits that employers predict their workers will be needed in an information economy their workers will need in an information economy.

The corporate model of reform pays little heed to other expectations of public schools: building just and tolerant communities, reducing distrust of one another and our shared institutions, safeguarding democratic ethics and introducing children to the cultural wisdom of the world. We are also witnessing the abandonment of many kinds of equality. Neither markets nor business ethics routinely put equality or fairness above profits. Whole groups of people will not fit the prevailing model of what it takes to be competitive in an educational market place in which competition is the guiding principle of improvement. Another disturbing trend is the anemic citizenship that economic justifications for schooling envision. Increasing the emphasis on individualism is likely to exacerbate a pattern of civic disengagement many already find disturbing in its scale and scope.

A Balancing Act to Reach a Healthy Equilibrium

We need a contemporary counter-movement to restore a healthy equilibrium of goals for our public schools. This movement would be grounded in a very different educational critique that rejects the metaphor of market (or management) failure and instead tackles the problems in our schools as symptoms of a widespread civic breakdown. The solutions to school failure would then hinge on common concerns, rather than rigorous individual competition and accountability. In addition to academic criteria, parents and reformers would craft student performance measures that reward active citizenship, tolerant and respectful behaviour, and cultural knowledge in the arts, history and languages. This reform movement, seeking equity and tolerance, would revitalise democratic institutions and not merely aim for more efficient production.

4

Violence in Schools: A World-wide Affair

In all countries, schools are magnets for strife in society. Dealing with these tensions calls for extreme caution, for fear of making matters worse. Violence in schools is a world wide problem: it exists in rich and poor countries alike. It's chiefly a male phenomenon, hitting a peak when boys turn 16 years old in some countries and 13 in others. Experts agree at least on one point: this violence cannot be pinned to a single cause. Instead, they point to complex patterns linked to family situations. Socio-economic conditions and teaching methods.

Tackling Segregation

But these are just indicators and do not justify any deterministic explanations. When researchers say that 10 to 20 per cent of risk factors are linked to single parent families, this suggests that 80 to 90 per cent of such families are not the source of any violence. A child from a slum area with a teenage mother or a father in jail will not automatically be violent! Likewise, experts say there is a 'hard core' of violent children—about five per cent of the total. One can found that this figure can vary between one and 11 per cent. The school itself can be an aggravating factor, through high staff turnover or 'ghetto classes' to which poorly-performing students are relegated. These 'hard core' groups, then, cannot be deemed 'inalterable'. On the contrary, something can be done about them.

Should they simply be expelled, as some advocate? Such a measure would only make their segregation and sense of exclusion worse. And they are, after all, at the root of the whole problem. The solution lies partly in developing customised projects, but most importantly, in strengthening economic social participation.

To put an end to school violence, we need a well-established state with the means to compensate for inequalities, a state that tries to re-establish diversity in neighbourhoods and schools, one that does not give up on the notion of justice for children, as some are demanding.

Passing the Torch

We should also try to lift schools out of their fortresses, so they do not become the symbol of a society that excludes people. Projects in the Netherlands, Brazil and the United States have shown that schools can be vibrant places that provide social, medical and cultural services to a neighbourhood.

In the Brazilian state of Minas Gerais, for example, there is a vocational school where elderly craftsmen teach their skills to teenagers. Such contact between generations can offer a very valuable social education. "It takes a village to educate a child", goes an effort an African proverb. Let's make an effort to seek out these opportunities, even in the most heartless cities.

5

Helping Your Child Learn

A one-syllable word begins the education process: 'Why?" Parents are always trying to answer that question. And that interaction between parent and child is the basis of much that children learn.

Teaching and learning are not mysteries that can happen only in school. They can also happen when parents and children do simple things together-things such as:

- Figure out whose socks are whose-sorting is a major function in maths and science;
- Cook a meal to learn science and good health;
- Tell each other a story as an important beginning for reading and writing; if the story is about the past, it's a way to interest a child in history;
- Plan a visit to a friend or relative for a personal connection with geography;
- Or play a game of hopscotch to develop counting and lifelong fitness.
- All children love their friends. So ask your child to describe his friend's appearance at the end of each school day. You can ask questions like: "What

outfit did he/she wear"? or "How did he/she do his/her hair"? This kind of routine query would encourage your child to observe his friend more minutely;

- If your child goes to school by bus, he can be asked to describe his route and point out certain landmarks namely colourful posters, traffic signals, large shops etc.

By doing things with their children, parents show that learning is fun and important—and that encourages children to study, learn, and stay in school.

Even on the discipline front, parents can help their children. Basic disciplinary principles must be tailored to each child and family. Before parents can become effective disciplinarians, they must first learn how to manage their own anger, solve problem situations and give and get support from others. Simple self-help techniques with or without professional support can help parents sharply reduce discipline problems.

Parents who are sensitive to their children's needs have more obedient children. Praise and love alone are not enough to instil good behaviour. Too much permissiveness hurts a child's efforts to develop self-control.

Behaviour problems should be reversed early. Waiting until the preteen-age years diminishes chances for success and puts children at higher risk for drug use and other problems.

Parents need to learn as many tricks of the trade as possible, including how to play with their children, Communicate with them, praise and reward them and also set limits for them, as well as how to handle misbehaviour using a variety of techniques.

All that parents need to help their children is a willingness to observe and learn with them, and, to take the time to nurture their natural curiosity.

6

Promotion of Higher Education in Research

The central role of Universities in the development of skills and knowledge as an absolute prerequisite for national development is undisputed. High education institutions have the responsibility for training a country's high level professional, technical and managerial personnel, they are to generate new knowledge through research and advanced scientific training, and they serve as agents in the transfer, adaptation and dissemination of knowledge. Higher education institutions also play an important role in contributing to the social cohesiveness of a nation and as a forum for constructive debates on development.

In a world economy which is heavily science-based and technology-driven higher education institutions, and particularly universities, have to provide such a competence which is indispensable for building a country's endogenous capacity for problem identification and problem solution through education combined with research. In India, however, universities have so far not been able to fulfil these roles, partly because the multiplicity of their missions is hardly compatible. Many critics of the universities in India consider them to be institutions of learning and research separated from the main stream of the economic and social needs of the population which they are supposed to serve. Most of them have not managed to reconcile the missions of providing country-oriented training and research and of being part of a wider international scientific community. Higher education institutions in many countries all over the world are confronted with a large scale and mostly uncontrolled expansion of the higher education sector and the concomitant growth expenditure against a background of dwindling financial resources to support such expansion. As a result of this expansion the quality of teaching and research has declined due to overcrowding, inadequate staffing, poor physical facilities and equipment. In addition universities often show a poor capacity for management and administration. This results in a low internal efficiency which amongst others is responsible for a rising graduate under or unemployment.

These deficiencies and a lack of national resources produce dependence on external sources particularly for research development. The low capacity for planning and management makes it difficult to properly employ external sources so that there may be pockets of good quality research in one field unrelated to neighbouring areas and not forming part of an endogenous research tradition.

Measures to be taken

The measures may be aimed specifically at increasing the efficiency of the system of higher education or of individual institutions by improving development relevance, quality and performance. More specifically are:

- to optimise and diversify the structure in line with the country's development requirements;

- to improve the capacity for efficient planning and administration;
- to diversify funding sources, with the aim of relieving the state budget;
- to improve access for talented students from all segements of society, giving special attention to the proportion of women studying.

At the level of individual institutions of higher education the aim should improve:

- education and training performance in the academic—scientific and vocational field;
- research and development capacities, especially in applied fields;
- the capacities to provide consultancy and services to contractors in state, business and industry, and society.

In order to achieve these objectives, it is necessary

- to train the academic, administrative and technical staff,
- to improve the infrastructure including central facilities and means of communications; and
- to increase efficiency by improving organisation.

The concept stresses the importance of measures designed to increase the efficiency of higher education in general through the strengthening of management capacities both at the system and at the institutions levels. This extends, inter alia, to the diversification of institutions of higher education in line with development needs, diversification in terms of funding, (including cost-sharing through fees) diversification in terms of study courses and practice-oriented training offered. Academic training at different levels for technical and executive staff.

New Areas of Promotion

The promotion of higher education institutions and subjects considered relevant for development (agriculture, natural sciences, engineering, medicine), the revised concept has to include areas such as the protection of the environment and resources, education, family planning and population policy.

In the wake of the political and economic reorientation taking place in many countries subjects like economics, law and social sciences are increasing in importance.

Prospects

Each country needs capacities which can produce the necessary analytical competence and research for generating information needed for designing and monitoring its development path. Institutions of higher education are essential in providing this competence. The responsibility for advanced education and the production of ideas and information should not be left to external donors. This may entail the concentration of resources, both internal and external, on one or only a few institutions of a country.

7

Wanted: A New Deal for the Universities

Higher education must meet new demands in order to turn out well-trained professionals instead of unemployed graduate. We are living through a period of profound historical change, marked by an on-going knowledge revolution. Society is changing far more quickly than the structures it has created and the universities are lagging behind these changes. They, and the educational system in general, continue to teach the use of static processes, forecasting models based on historical experience and the memorising of solutions to already solved problems.

Higher education systems in both North and South are in crisis, both quantitatively and qualitatively. Naturally the developing countries are the hardest hit, both in terms of available resources and levels of student enrollment.

Is the crisis due to a shortage of funds alone? Does the fact that the countries of the North invest ten times more per student than those of the South mean that graduates from the former are ten times better trained? Common sense says yes. But in most cases the answer is no. Generally speaking, university education has failings all over the world, in some cases because it is an offspring of a wasteful society, indifferent to the resources with which that society provides them.

The Missing Link Between Education and the World of Work

In the United States, for example, many teachers and researches come from developing societies which should theoretically have given them a less sound training than that provided by the immense academic and financial resources of the United States system. But this is not the case: they compete professionally and scientifically, with no major problems. In many areas the results of university training are comparable.

Professionals move around because they need jobs and want to work in the best possible working conditions. There are, for example, almost 30,000 African Ph.Ds working in Europe and North America, and thousands of Latin American and Asian professionals working in the United States. By the beginning of the 1990s about a million professionals had emigrated to the developed countries over the previous three decades, and the figure has increased considerably in the last five years. While the number of opportunities and access to them are uneven, there is little difference between North and South as regards quality; nor is the availability of funding the only basis for improving the system.

The problem is that post-secondary training today is diploma-driven. It is based on rigid study programmes and is changing at a rate which takes little or no account of the speed of knowledge accumulation. This is despite the fact that today's graduate professional needs to have followed a flexible curriculum and must be a problem solver, extremely adaptable to new processes and technologies generously endowed with creativity and firmly inclined towards lifelong learning, as is clear from the studies on skilled labour done by industrialised countries and from numerous OECD studies.

A recent study of the relationship between higher education and the labour market observes that there appears to be no connection between the increase in professionals' level of knowledge and changes on the labour market. Although the market undoubtedly demands basic skills and knowledge, it is attaching increasing importance to the emotional and psychological attitudes of future employees.

Although post-secondary education is clearly associated with higher personal incomes, lower unemployment and greater opportunities to climb the social ladder, unemployment rates for people with higher education qualifications continue to be high in both North and South. Graduates unemployment in Europe, for example, varies between 1.4 per cent and 16.6 per cent depending on the country. What's more, many graduates are working in jobs outside their field of training. The increase in graduate unemployment in the developing countries is largely due to the drastic fall in demand from the major employer of graduates—the state—as a result of international competition and new political and economic approaches. The private sector is in no position to absorb the supply of surplus graduates. World Bank studies carried out in Asia, the Middle East, North Africa and certain Latin American countries show that graduate unemployment is increasing.

All the same, higher education cannot be held wholly responsible for graduate unemployment nor for the correlation that should exist between training, study programmes and demand for labour. It is often said that higher education is failing to provide training in the activities required by the market, but the market is often incapable of adequately anticipating the type of professionals it is going to need.

A survey conducted in Florida (USA) among multinationals in the high-tech and services sectors revealed companies that were unable to identify the professional qualities that would be required within ten years and, in many cases, within five years. This is not surprising, in view of the spectacular rise of the Internet between 1994 and 1998 which caught many hardware and software firms unaware. It is in information technology that redundancies and high unemployment levels are occurring, because systems are constantly changing and because of strategic mergers between the major companies.

Another example of the difficulty of making reliable predictions concerns those made by the European Community and the US Government regarding the type of jobs that would be needed at the beginning of the new century. These predictions were inaccurate: what had been forecast to occur after 2001 actually came about in the last 1980s and early 1990s.

It can be said, however, that professional training over the coming years will focus on areas such as high-tech electronics, information technology, aqua-culture, agro-energy, biotechnology and energy physics. Jobs in information and communication systems will require new qualifications which will have to be continually updated. The service sector will experience spectacular growth in the field of leisure and recreation because of the reduction in working hours. New professions in the human sciences such as 'ludicadology', incorporating psychology, pedagogy, information science and the technology of education, play and creativity programmes, will replace the old single-discipline approach.

In short, the great occupational change looming ahead will call for increased interdisciplinarity, revitalisation of the disciplines related to thick and aesthetics and sweeping changes in the attitudes of teachers and students: for the professional of the future, education will be a lifelong process, and education and work will go hand in hand.

The great challenge will thus be to create a stable relationship between higher education and society through strategic alliances with the production system designed to promote participation by all sectors of the economy in the university's basic and applied research programmes and by production-sector specialists in university teaching.

The problems of the university are also those of society, and so are the responsibilities. This raises the question of the university's specific culture, especially the teacher-student relationship. Planning is currently based above all on the teaching staff, which is more corporatist than academic. Physical spaces, salary scales, curricula, structures and time tables are more closely geared to the needs of the teacher than of teaching. This is the case all over the world.

More serious still, this teacher-centred culture is giving way to one that is even more dangerous for the survival of university education: and administration-centred culture. This would mean an education system dominated by bureaucrats and the kind of management structures which would place an institution whose function is to produce and disseminate knowledge on the same footing as a detergent factory or a multinational travel agency.

But no strategy for change can work unless higher education adapts to the challenge of the knowledge explosion. It is vital that course content should be geared to what learners 'must know' and not to what teachers 'know' or 'think they know'. This will force teachers into a permanent renal of theories, techniques and processes, keeping up with knowledge produced both inside and outside the university. Higher education is evolving towards a model in which lecturers and students will be permanent learners and where curricula will be drawn up on the basis of innovation, fresh knowledge and the latest teaching and learning technologies. Above all the university must teach people to think to use common sense and to give free rein to the creative imagination.

8

Shaking the Ivory Tower

Universities have changed radically to keep pace with modern life. Now where are they heading in this high-speed age? In the past half century higher education has been transformed from a privilege conferred on social and political elites to a mass activity available to whole populations. This process began in the United States in the 1940s and 1950s, spread to most of Western Europe and many other developed countries during the 1960s and 1970s and in the past two decades has become a global phenomenon. In the next half century it well accelerate, leading perhaps to the replacement of 'higher education' (still an elite-ish category despite its expansion) by extended systems of 'lifelong learning'.

The key to this transformation has been the expansion of secondary education. For example, in all but two countries of the OECD (Organisation for Economic Cooperation and Development) at least two thirds of young people now complete upper secondary education, and so are eligible to enter higher education. The result has been a dramatic increase in enrolment rates in higher education. In Chile the total number of students has grown from

131,000 in 1978 to 235,000 in 1988 and to 343,000 in the mid 1990s. Even in the United States, the pioneer of mass-access higher education where very high secondary education completion rates had already been achieved before 1970, the student population has continued to grow, from 11 million in 1978 to 13 million in 1988 and now to more than 14 million.

Two forces have driven up completion rates in upper secondary education and enrolment rates in higher education. The first has been democratisation. As late as 1945 high levels of social, and hence educational, inequality persisted even in democratic countries, and much of the world remained in the grip of colonial and totalitarian powers. In North America, Western Europe and Australasia democratisation typically took the form of the development of 'welfare states', in which there was an increase in public expenditure on education, housing, health and social security that was sustained over more than three decades after the end of the Second World War.

More recently, as renewed emphasis has been placed on the market even in social policy, the rise of consumerism has continued to fuel demands for increased higher education opportunities. The older idea of education as a civil entitlement has been compounded by newer notions of free access to the education marketplace. Far from arresting the advance to mass higher education, consumerism has accelerated it in most developed countries. As traditional forms of social differentiation based on class, gender and ethnic origin have been eroded by democratisation and by market forces, new forms based on educational certification have become more important. In many developed countries the middle class and the 'graduate class' have tended to coalesce.

In much of Asia and Africa democratisation took the form of decolonisation. In newly independent countries the energy originally generated in liberation struggles against the colonial powers was directed into a wider struggle to create fairer and more equal successor societies. Education was central to this struggle. The result has been a rapid increase in higher education enrolment—for example, in Tunisia from barely 2,000 students at the time of independence to more than 100,000 today. That process continues.

However, the relationship between democratisation and the development of higher education has been less straightforward in developing countries. Despite very rapid rates of expansion the 'metropolitan' influences of the former colonial powers have lingered more stubbornly in higher education than at other levels of education. This is partly due to the continued influence of associations between universities in the British Commonwealth as well as those between francophone universities.

Partly because of these lingering 'metropolitan' models and partly because levels of participation are still lower than in developed countries, many African or Asian universities have remained more elite institutions than higher education institutions in North America and Europe. Also, as economic conditions have worsened in some developing countries, the competition between primary and higher education sharpened in the post-independence years as both were seen as equally important priorities. This competition was often reinforced by the intervention of the World Bank.

The Second force driving up higher education enrolments has been the changing nature of the labour market. Traditional occupations have become comparatively less significant, while new service occupations, which often require graduate-level skills, have become more important.

Skill requirements have become more sophisticated. Jobs once done by unskilled or semi-skilled workers are now undertaken by technicians; and those which as recently as the 1980s were taken by technicians are now likely to be filled by graduates. The capital invested for every worker has more than doubled in the past 20 years. Even in occupations where there is less evidence that skills contents have changed significantly, university graduates are now employed in much larger numbers, partly to enhance the social status of these occupations and partly to compete in a graduate-dominated labour market. Healthcare is a good example. Once doctors were the only graduates; today, many para-medical workers are also trained in higher education.

The second form taken by the economic driver has been the growing conviction that national success now depends on economic competitiveness which, in the context of a knowledge-based economy, depends in turn on an adequate supply of human capital. Knowledge is now seen as the key economic resource.

This analysis may be exaggerated; raw materials are still very important in national economies and the global economy. But it has become pervasive and persuasive. The naive and linear theories of human capital popular a generation ago which postulated a direct link between investment in education and economic growth may have been challenged; some forms of higher education are now as likely to be labelled consumption as investment goods. Nevertheless, the discourse of the 'Knowledge Society' has become even more powerful.

The impact of democratisation and economic competitiveness on higher education has been immense. First, the expansion of student numbers has made the cost of higher education a significant element within national budgets for the first time. A number of important consequences has folowed from this—the opportunity, and incentive, to compare the value of investing in different levels of education; increasing demands that universities are run as efficiently as possible (compromising their traditional autonomy from the state and the market); lower unit costs as budgets have been trimmed (which may have undermined higher education's claim to represent academic excellence). Second, higher education systems have emerged that embrace not only traditional universities but also non-university institutions. Two effects have been produced. One is that the ethos of the traditional university has been eroded; it no longer stands in glorious isolation. The other is that institutional differentiation has been encouraged, whether through active state planning or in response to markets for teaching and research.

The prospects for the next half century are for an acceleration of both drivers—to include access to higher education among the basic entitlements enjoyed by citizens in democratic societies; and to 'put knowledge to work' in order to generate wealth and to improve the quality of life. The prospects for higher education during the same period are also relatively easy to predict—increased efficiency (which is likely to include growing pressure to make students contribute more to the cost of their higher education); greater accountability, although more probably in a 'market' than a 'planning' mode as even the state redefines its role as the purchaser of higher education services, more differentiation, both between and within higher education institutions, as they struggle to identify market niches; and possibly-growing demands that higher education become more relevant as instrumental considerations triumph over idealistic ones.

However, the future may be more complex than the past. In the second half of the 20th century the encounter between high education and society has been comparatively straightforward. Although dynamic, society has presented a familiar enough face. It was characterised by a combination of bureaucratic rationailty and secular (and liberal) individualism. The beneficence of science and technology was uncontested. The dominant economic model was of large scale industry, or analogous organisations in the corporate and public sectors. Although rapidly evolving, concepts and categories like 'career' and 'profession' remained valid. Higher education too was familiar enough. Despite the great expansion of student numbers and its adoption of novel roles, the university continued to be recognisable as such. Other types of higher education institution have been deeply influenced by university values and practices.

In the first half of the 21st century both society and higher education may become problematical and so contested categories. Some of these uncertainties are already emerging. Once firm demarcations between public and private domains, whether in terms of the balance between the state and the market or between social 'spaces' and individual desires; between producers and users; between investment and consumption; between work and leisure are becoming increasingly fuzzy in the emerging post-industrial society. Wealth is being generated by the production of 'symbolic' as well as—or more than—material goods. Value is created by design, sales, marketing, service rather than by primary production. Institutions of all kinds, civic and corporate, are being challenged by the rise of adaptable and flexible organisations, made possible by advances in communications and information technology.

The force of globalisation amounts to much more than round-the-clock-round-the world financial markets or an emerging international division of labour; it is not only undermining nation states but also reconfiguring time and space to produce global intimacies, again with the help of the information revolution. Social identities are no longer moulded by the 'givens' of religion, class and gender, or by positions within the occupational structure, as they have been since the advent of the industrial revolution in Europe two centuries ago. Instead they are being subsumed by a process of individualisation in which life-styles rather than life-chances predominate.

Higher education will have not only to continue to satisfy the predictable demands for democratic entitlement and socio-economic utility with which it is familiar, but also to cope with the consequences of these new uncertainties. These may include; new curricula that emphasise style and images at the expense of skills and information; recategorisation of higher education as a playful, even selfish, activity; a tighter link between experience of higher education and social esteem, submergence of the universal, but also particular, values characteristic of the traditional university by anomic globalisation; threats to the scientific tradition and methods, from the 'risk society' from subjectivisation and from demands that other knowledge traditions are accorded equal respect.

The universities of the 21st century, therefore, may have to face two ways. They will have to continue to pay attention to the democratisation and the 'knowledge society' agendas, which are likely both to be subsumed in a larger 'lifelong learning' agenda. Their ability to sustain current levels of public funding and to satisfy their student-customers will depend on their success in this respect. It will not be easy. There is a danger that the essence of higher education will be lost if it succumbs to unconstrained populism. If this happens, the 'quality' of the university will disappear and with it perhaps its distinctiveness and so its utility and marketability. Similarly in the knowledge society of the future the university will face new rivals because all organisations will need to become 'learning organisations'. These rivals strength will be increased if the superiority of universal science is successfully challenged.

But universities will also have to address the new agendas of the 'death' of work (land graduate careers?), of new social movements (and the erosion of individual enlightenment), of globalisation and virtulisation (and the undermining of academic community?); of 'alternative' knowledge traditions and, perhaps even, anti-cognitive values with the undermining of 'objective' science and further erosion of a common intellectual culture.

9

Wiring Up the Ivory Towers

Prestigious universities are forging alliances to conquer a share of the e-learning market and stand up to virtual competitors just like airline companies, universities around the world are forming partnerships and consortia in response to the pressures of globalisation. The World Education Market held in Vancouver was a timely sign; the fair, expressly organised to foster relations between universities, training providers, software companies and representatives from nations with large education needs attracted participants from over 60 countries.

This race to 'partner up' is fuelled by a number of factors. In most industrialised countries, government funding for higher education has decreased, forcing institutions to look for new markets either to subsidise campus programmes or just to remain viable. There is a growing need for lifelong learning as 'jobs for life' vanish and the information society drastically reduces the shelf-life of almost any educational qualification. Technological developments, increasingly necessary for learners in all fields to master, offer ever more innovative tools for supporting e-learning.

For business, online learning is 'the' new market opportunity with the need for re-training and professional updating predicted to crease an $ 11.5 billion industry by 2003. Business is better able to develop and maintain the technological infrastructure necessary to run large online systems and everyone, including the universities, recognises that it takes robust telecommunications technology to deliver education and training on the scale demanded.

As host of companies has sprung up to help universities shape and package courses for online presentation, while network providers are jockeying for position to deliver online education.

The United States is the undisputed leader in the field, promoting governments in the U.K., Canada and Australia to commission being eroded by U.S. ventures turned global, Canada and the U.K. are in the early stages of setting up their own virtual universities. But what has become clear is that the conservative and labyrinthine decision-making processes which characterise most university procedures are being jolted by a race to get a share of the lifelong learning market.

So far, the most common approach for universities to break into the e-learning universe has been to develop courses specifically for a corporate partner or to form alliances among themselves. Universities 21, a company incorporated in the U.K., is a network of 18 leading universities in ten countries.

Very often, prestigious universities has stayed clear of going fully online, seeing a danger to their brand name. Many are limiting their offering to continuing education programmes and/or non-degree courses, and more often than not, they are aiming at the corporate market. One Company unext.com, has partnered with first-class institutions such as the University of Columbia (U.S.) and the London School of Economics to create online courses marketed under the name Cardean University. Their target: the Fortune 500 companies as well as individual adults. They've managed to attract Nobel Laureates to design courses and the universities have formed spin-off for-profit companies specifically to develop online programmes. This facilities the commercialisation of software and other products, and is a way to take a commercial approach to continuing and professional studies without compromising the University's standing.

Then there are the freestanding for profit virtual universities which are arousing the ire of institutions that have prided themselves on a long history of public service. The most quoted exemplar is a Phoenix University, the largest private outfit in the U.S. Now owned by the Apollo Group, it operates the country's largest online programme with 12,200 students. The university tracks students progress and contacts those who don't submit assignments on time or fail to enrol in subsequent courses. Many critics question Phoenix's blatant commercialisation, but few doubt the university's impact on continuing professional development provision.

Although e-learning is in its infancy, its impact can already by gauged. New providers are coming on the market all the time and the trend is accelerating to the point of upsetting universities virtual monopoly in educational accreditation. An Information Technology training course offered or accredited by Microsoft has undoubtedly become more valuable than a Bachelor of Science from a renowned university.

The more consumerist the approach of the education provider, the more what is taught is influenced by demand. MBAs dominate e-learning provision and IT courses are a close second. While the new consumer/learner demands flexibility, choice and just-in-time learning opportunities, suppliers will inevitably arise who are focused on meeting the demand at the expense of quality and value. And is the consumer really the best judge of what course material to choose? Education is a more complex 'product' than toothpaste or washing powder. A totally consumer driven education market is unlikely to be in society's best interest in the long term. The commercialisation of education usually goes hand-in-hand with desegregation: course design, delivery, tutoring assessment and accreditation may be carried out by different organisations. Students might study courses or modules from different universities or providers and then put themselves forward for examination and accreditation by yet another institution. While most academics loathe marking assignments, they regard this scenario with horror, and blame commercialisation for the demise of the community of scholars' concept of a university. The death of the 'course' has also been predicated, with learners—especially corporate and on-the job learners—demanding short study modules. What then happens to the ability to get an overview of a field when learning consists of the students selecting a whole series of unconnected learning 'bites'? Learners will be 'zapping' between short sequences or presentations much as they do between television channels.

But while some faculty view e-learning with alarm, technology-based learning is where most of the pedagogical innovation is taking place in universities. Multimedia learning resources and interactive simulations are being developed for the web. Collaborative learning activities, new forms of online assessment and small group teaching technologies are making online courses more stimulating, interactive and attractive than many face-to-face taught courses.

Despite 'doom and gloom scenarios', most moderate observers of the scene see a continued future for the campus university, especially at the undergraduate level, while e-learning will above all cater to adult professional and independent learners. Some commercialisation of education is good if it fosters innovation, concern for quality and responsiveness to consumer demands. But if some is good, more is not necessarily better! Not in education at least.

10

Management Training in India

In the developing world as a whole, and also in India it can be recognised that a wide 'managerial gap' exists between the demand for and supply of indigenous management talent at nearly all levels. This gap constitutes a major constraint in achieving better economic, social and agricultural development.

The importance of development effective managers is today widely recognised. To achieve economic, social, and human development a capable and talented cadre of managers must be developed in each country.

There are several reasons for the paucity of managerial skills in India. Some of these include the rapid expansion of the public sector through the increase in development programmes, the tendency to focus on technical and professional education training rather than administration and management, and the inability of so much of the education and training to produce capable managers.

Since Independence India has invested heavily in education and training. Training in management is a complex process. Although the importance of 'good' management to the success of specific development projects as well as to long term national development has been well recognised, the nature of 'good' management is culturally specific. Over the past forty years, the development of management skills in India has been mainly treated as a problem of the transfer of techniques. Some Western countries, by virtue of their level of economic development, were supposed to possess know how about management techniques which could be transferred to other countries lacking this know how. Future managers and management trainers from less economically advanced countries were sent to school in more developed countries; management experts from these more developed countries acted as consultants and trainers in less developed countries. Such persons taught and learned the only management concepts then known—those developed in the West's more industrialised nations. However, India should develop its own indigenous sources of adaptive managerial theory and practice instead of imitating western concepts.

After the period of formal colonisation an impressive number of management training institutions have been established in India. At the moment, India is not in short supply of management training institutions.

It seems undeniable that management training institutes in India potentially have a huge capability to contribute to the economic development of India.

However a close look at the programmes of Indian management training institutions and the contribution they give to the development of management reveals that their programmes are mainly focussed upon improving the public sector in their regions, while the private sector is left uncatered for.

The public sector is important in stimulating development in India for the coming years the public sector will continue to be the most important employer in India.

Managers that deal with the public sector need a number of fundamentally different management skills from those that deal with the entrepreneurial sector. Among other qualities, public service managers must be able to deal effectively with socio-economic policymaking and be able to undertake planning and budgeting, they need to know how to get work done by their staff, they need to know how to delegate work. On the other hand, new entrepreneurs need to know how to get started in business, how to write and implement a business plan, how to manage and market a new product development process, how to establish licensing arrangements, and so on.

Management training institutes need to be adjusted to new training and teaching methods developed on the basis of current insights in the roots of the crisis in India and mechanisms to overcome these. Some training institutes are making progress in their adjustment process.

Revitalisation of the management training infrastructure in order to establish and restore quality seems to be one of the main elements. If the process of adjustment is taken seriously by the management of the Indian management training institutions, there is certainly a need for some selective expansion of training programmes. If the focus is shifted for training exclusively directed towards the public sector to training likewise for the entrepreneurial sector some expansion is needed.

What is drastically needed is a re-conceptualisation of management training, expanding the concept to include a large variety and multiplicity of learning activities outside of formal classroom training sessions. There are a wide variety of management training approaches and methods available for enhancing managerial talent such as on-the-job training, action training and non-formal training.

There has emerged some widespread agreement during the last years about what might be done to advance concerted action in India to create sustainable development. Management training institutions should contribute to this action:

Development must be Human Centered Process

There is widespread recognition now that people are both the ends and the means of development and, therefore, that programmes of human-centered development, of food security, and of employment must be placed on center-stage of any economic development, strategy, both in the short run and in the long run. Management training institutions should play an important role in human resources development and provide public and private sector officials with skills and knowledge to afford their people with minimum food requirements, to increase the possibilities of basic education, and to improve primary health care.

A Strategy of Human Development will not Succeed Unless Production Growth is Restored

The restoration of agricultural and industrial prosperity is necessary both for the achievement of macro economic objectives—export earning, import savings, tax revenues, etc.—and of social objectives—employment creation, productivity increases of poor peasants, financial resources for education, health, etc.

In this whole area of increasing productivity management training institutions should give public sector officials and private sector employees skills and knowledge about how to increase productivity.

India has these days investment policies to attract foreign investments, however, top executives in both the public and private sectors lack the skills, knowledge and attitudes to implement these policies. These policies could have a major impact upon the environment in India of which the executives might not be aware. These training areas could form a challenge to management training institutions.

India's Development Efforts will come to Naught Unless Governance is Improved

This clearly raises very sensitive issues. There is widespread agreement now that without improvements in governance, development will prove to be neither equitable nor sustainable. Good governance is based on the observance of certain principles such as accountability of government leaders, transparency in the use of public funds, responsiveness of government to popular aspirations and room for people to participate in all spheres of social and economic life to produce, to organise their mutual assistance, and to express their views on development decisions affecting their existence.

Management training institutions should provide government employees with skills to improve their governance.

11

For a Broader Approach to Education

In our rapidly changing world, literacy should be seen as an important evolutionary variable in every society. For the further a society progresses, the more it needs to adjust and adapt to new demands and pressures, so that literacy is lifelong necessity for all.

Literacy, in the broad sense, is the foundation for life skills, ranging from basic oral and written communication to the ability to solve scientific and social problems. Today it involves much more than the acquisition of 3 Rs. And a limited set of traditional skills. It is linked with the changing demands of life in a given socio-cultural context.

This means that local communities should be fully involved in defining the content of literacy programmes. The local dimension of literacy is extremely important not only for accommodating the real needs of learners, but also for taking into account the linguistic and cultural realities of multicultural societies. For in the end, only the learners actually decide what they need to learn.

Building Bridges Between Cultures

Most literacy specialist have accepted this broader, more

dynamic and culturally sensitive stance. It marks a long overdue acknowledgement of the positive role that local language and cultures can play in removing some of the serious pedagogical and psychological hurdles often encountered by learners, it is the only way to ensure the relevance and authority of literacy work.

Any one can insist here on the importance of multilingual education. Today education is as much about learning to live together as learning to know, to do and to be. Yet we cannot live together if our possibilities of expression are limited to a single linguistic frame. This is often at the root of problems encountered in multicultural societies. Of course, inequality in all its forms is a major factor. But internal conflicts often have purely cultural causes. It is more difficult for people to forge links with each other when they cannot communicate linguistically.

Yet children learn languages easily—much more so than the adults who take the decisions. We need to take much greater advantage of this fact. Children are expected to store too much information in their 'hard memory'—much of its frankly useless! Giving them language skills provides them with bridges between cultures, enabling them to grow up without the debilitating sense that other cultures are lien. It is our task to try to ensure that education at all levels, and particularly basic education, promotes multilinguilism. And we must invest in such education, since to do so is to invest in peace.

It is also important to remind ourselves that literacy is not a neutral process which can be applied in all situations, all the time, regardless of social and economic realities. Such a narrow concept of literacy ignores its critical role at a tool of empowerment. One can treat adult learners as empty vessels waiting to be filled with predetermined bodies of knowledge disconnected from their social experience. Literacy must provide space of intellectual development, motivations for learning and a sense of self-esteem, if it is to be a genuine education for empowerment.

Bringing Adult Education into the Mainstream

Many individuals and families around the world are facing unexpected changes in the pattern of their daily lives, disrupting their plans for the future. The demands on educational services are increasing dramatically, especially in countries where the state is the main provider of education for children and adults. In today's world, we cannot afford a short-sighted approach which, in effect, excludes adult education from the mainstream of the education system, even after the concept of life long learning has been accepted as a framework for educational policy.

Literacy programmes must be given the priority they deserve. Lifelong learning for all requires quality adult education and literacy programmes with qualified personnel, relevant teaching programmes, appropriate post-literacy materials and decent facilities. We must ask ourselves whether we recently are prepared to make the necessary; investments in adult education and literacy to ensure universal access to the types of programmes needed to reach the targets of education for all.

If we truly believe in lifelong learning, and if we seriously believe in redressing the balance of learning in our societies, then we should seek to develop in every country an open and more enabling system of education, breaking with past concepts of education as something which happens to people between the ages of six and twenty and which only the privileged of few were entitled to. Synergy has to be created between formal and non-formal education programmes.

A case in point is the family literacy concept. We all know that the continuing education of parents, particularly when they are illiterate or under-educated, can contribute very effectively to their children's success in school. In fact the family literacy approach is one of the most effective ways of breaking the cycle of inter-generational illiteracy. Education and training policies should include all types of learning, whether it takes place in a school, in the workplace or at home. There should be more innovation and creativity in using methods and approaches.

12

Policy Researchers and Policy Makers: Never the Twain Shall Meet?

In every corner of the planet, researchers are gathering and analysing information on vital issues of sustainable development. But how do they know that their findings will actually be used in policy decisions that create positive change? Researchers and decision makers see the world, and their roles in it, in very different ways. What creates this divide between the two communities and what can be done to bridge the gap?

'Demand-Side' Challenges: Policy in the Making

By its nature, the policy making process constrains decision makers from effectively expressing demands for research. Rigorous research requires a clear definition of a problem and the variables to be measured. But the objectives of government policies and programmes tend to be loosely defined and even contradictory. Many decisions are reached through a multilateral bargaining process in which it is difficult to obtain consensus on anything more than broad statements of principle. These bargains might break down if the costs and tradeoffs involved were exposed by a research project.

Inertia and more urgent priorities mean that governments tend to think about changing policies only when time and funding have run out. At that point, it is too late for research. Furthermore, it is only after a programme has been established and a clientele created that an effective demand exists for research. For these reasons, policy implementation tends to precede rather than follow research.

Even if there is a need for research, they may not be a single agency responsible for the policy decision bargaining. When a client agency does request advice, there is no guarantee that it will turn out to be the appropriate audience for the results (*e.g.* a study done for the ministry of education might find that student performance would be improved by better nutrition).

Finally, governments are often afflicted with too much information, which senior policy makers have little time to absorb.

'Supply Side' Challenges of Academic Research

Problems also exist in the research community that supplies information and analysis. University research usually takes a long time to yield results. It is often highly critical, without suggestions for action, but fitting the self-image of many academics a gadflies. In academia, a state of conflicting views and information is normal. But potential clients find their confidence undermined when two studies reach opposite conclusions.

Academics often search for general laws and patterns that reveal phenomena of greater theoretical and long run importance than highly specific observations. Policy makers, however, want answers to the specific problems they face, even if such 'small' problems do not interest researchers.

While policy makers tend to emphasize distributional concerns (*i.e.* winners and losers) and the number of people affected, economists—frequent advisors to government—emphasize efficiency and financial costs and benefits. Owing partly to the vagueness of many programme goals, policy makers tend to assess performance in terms of inputs rather than improvements in health). They also weigh losses more heavily than gains, since "a policy that hurts five people and helps five, produces five enemies and five ingrates".

Finally, the issue of compensation is critical to policy makers; for economists it is usually an afterthought. Economists tend to find a solution satisfactory if, in theory, the losers could be compensated. To push a policy change through, policy makers must usually ensure that they will be compensated, and have mechanisms to do so.

Impact Down the Road

The gap between demand and supply for research appears rather large. But this view may be too pessimistic, mainly because it uses narrow definitions of research and policy impact. Research is more than a set of data and policy impact may accumulate imperceptibly but with real effect over many years. The contribution of social science research is perhaps less in proposing specific solutions to well-defined problems, than in defining the problems and providing an array of concepts and methods for analysis.

Problem definition can take many forms. It can mean detecting problems from patterns in data, such as a trend toward worsening income distribution. It can also change the way society thinks about issues. Largely because of research, the informal sector now tends to be seen as a potential force for development, rather than a symptom of backwardness.

The most significant contribution of social science research may be in generating ideas and ideologies, which history shows can be very powerful.

What to do?

How, then, can researchers and the agencies that sponsor them increase the social relevance and impact of research? Since both the problem-solving and the conceptual impacts are important, research programmes should be designed to provide both by developing an understanding of basic behavioural relationships and a thorough knowledge of the data. This can then be tapped to provide short-term policy advice.

Donors have an important role to play in supporting theoretical research, although they are sometimes reluctant to do so. The distinction between 'theoretical' and 'empirical' is in no sense equivalent to 'useless and 'useful'. A plausible, variable theory about how farmers respond to increases in crop prices, or savings to changes in interest rates, is of obvious relevance to poverty and can be very useful.

Greater attention should go to publicising findings and donors should be prepared to finance conferences, books, working papers, abstracts and the like. Researchers should convey their findings in language intelligible to practitioners, putting themselves into policy makers' shoes when doing so. Among the recommendations made by successful policy advisors are the following.

- ❒ learn about the history of the issue by researching previous arguments, interest groups, areas of disagreement and data gaps;
- ❒ get into the debate early before positions harden;
- ❒ explain which groups will be affected by the proposed measures and suggest ways to compensate those negatively affected;

- do not propose measures that are technically optimal but too complex or costly for an agency to administer; and

- keep it simple. Emphasize the decision at hand, the underlying problem, and options to solve it. Minimise methodology, jargon and equations.

In the research domain, there is no single recipe for policy impact. Luck and persistence, along with good science, are vital ingredients.

13

Population Growth and Education

In contrast to the food supply challenge posed by the coming wave of population growth, the global need for teachers and classrooms will rise very slowly in the next half-century. In many countries, the school-age population is increasing much less rapidly than the overall national population, the trend illustrates that growth rates typically differ from different age strata of the population. It also shows that declining birth rates can take decades to move through an entire population.

At the global level, for example, total population is projected to increase by 54 per cent between 2000 and 2050, but the number of children aged 5 to 14 will grow by only 6 per cent. And of the world's largest countries-accounting for 60 per cent of global population in 1995—will actually begin to see decreases in the number of children aged 5 to 14 by 2015; for several of these countries, the decline in this age group has already begun. These countries will need fewer classrooms and teachers to educate the youngest members of society (assuming they maintain current class size and student-teacher ratios).

Plenty of nations, however, still have increasing child-age populations. Where countries have not acted to stabilize population, the base of the national population pyramid continues to expand, and pressures on the educational system will be severe. In the world's 10 fastest-growing countries, for example, most of which are in Africa and the Middle East, the child-age population will increase in average 93 per cent over the next half-century. Africa as a whole will see its school-age population grow by 75 per cent through 2040.

The rapid growth in African populations is especially worrisome because of the extra burden it imposes in a region already lagging in education. Only 56 per cent of Africans south of the Sahara are literate, compared with 71 per cent for all developing countries. Few African countries have universal primary education, and secondary education reaches only 4-5 per cent of African children. Educating today's children is challenge enough; the addition of another three students for every four already there will require heroic investments in education. But the alternative is grim: without additional investments in education, today's average student-teacher ratio of 42 in sub-Saharan Africa will reach 75 by 2040.

Many countries will be challenged to increase funding for education while ensuring that other worthy sectors also receive the support they need. With 900 million illiterate adults in the world, the case for a renewed commitment to education is easy to make. But competiting for these funds are the 840 million chronically hungry and the 1.2 billion without access to a decent toilet.

The budget stresses on governments attempting to meet these basic needs would clearly be reduced with smaller populations. Mozambique and Lesotho, for example, both met the UNESCO benchmark for investment in education in 1992, six per cent of gross domestic product—and the two countries economies were roughly equal in size. Yet because Mozambique has many times the population of Lesotho, spending per child in Lesotho is about nine times higher than in Mozambique. For the majority of countries who do not meet the UNESCO funding standard, many of whom all fall short in providing other basic services, a decline in population pressure could help substantially to meet all of their social goals.

If national education systems begin to stress life-long learning for a rapidly changing world, as recommended by a 1998 UNESCO report on education in the twenty-first century, then extensive provision for adult education will be necessary, affecting even those countries with shrinking childgage populations, such a development means that countries that started population stabilisation programmes earliest will be in the best position to educate their entire citizenry.

14

No Progress Without A Secular Society

Every day, women continue to be victims of rape, trafficking, acid-throwing, dowry deaths and other kinds of torture. At the opening of this new century, women are still not considered as equal human beings in many parts of the world, Religion and patriarchy continue to have an all-encroaching hold on their lives, maintaining and justifying their age-old oppression. In some South Asian Societies, this hold is even increasing.

I do not believe that there can be real equality in a society dominated by religion. Western countries speak repeatedly about the necessity of economic development to alleviate poverty. But this is not enough. Some oil rich countries may be economically developed, but women are deprived of all rights. The supremacy of religion is incompatible with freedom of expression, women's rights and democracy. This is why I see religion as the main enemy of women's development.

We have to act on several fronts at once. First of all, improving access to education. In a society like Bangladesh, 80 per cent of women are illiterate. For centuries women have been taught they are the slaves of men. It is very hard to change their minds, to make them aware of their oppression, to give them a sense of their independence. This educational effort has to go hand in hand with a secular feminist movement in society. Such movements have to start within the country and they cannot take hold when people are uneducated and unaware of their oppression. I'm not sure you can accomplish much from outside, except to expose in the media the atrocities women in all too many countries face in their day to day lives.

In some countries, this movement is emerging, but very timidly, and it has a slim margin of maneuver. It has the uphill task of fighting for the repeal of religious laws and the introduction of a uniform civil code. So far, it tends to be constituted by a few individual feminists who are forced to be diplomatic, to compromise with fundamentalists, be they men or women. But they are trying to change the system, step by step, and it will take a very long time. People are not yet ready to do away with religious laws that impact upon every aspect of society, from education and health to the workplace and the home.

For women's status to change, we also need enlightened leaders who believe in equality. In countries of South Asia women with a strong voice do not have the support of political leaders, whether they be men or women. Look at the countries in which women are in politics, or even heads of state. Does it follow that women in those countries are emancipated? Because of long-standing vested interests, such leaders continue to back measures that oppress women. They are not ideologically committed to changing these conditions. In South Asia, most of the women who become heads of state are religious, and like men, they adhere to the religious objectives of the establishment. Until a society is not based on religion and women and considered equal to men before the law, I do not think that politics will advance the cause of women.

Until a society is not based on religion and women are considered equal to men before the law, I do not think that politics will advance the cause of women. In Western countries, women are educated, they are treated equally, they have access to jobs. In these conditions, their participation in politics has a meaning.

Education, a secular feminist movement, and leaders—both men and women—committed to equality and justice. This is what it will take to change the dire conditions which too many women still face today. It will take a very long time, but we are here to work towards that end.

15

Solving the Unemployment Problem by Looking Beyond the Job

If you had a job, you worked; if you didn't, you didn't. Having a job meant being employed by an organisation in a clearly-defined and stable occupational role, with duties, hours, rates of pay and promotion all more or less standardised. But the job—in that meaning of the world—is a social invention, and a fairly recent one.

The job—the kind that you had, or hoped to get—became a central fixture of life. Its importance was great because it served many needs. For managers and efficiency experts, job assignments were the key to assembly-line manufacturing. For union organisers, jobs protected the rights of workers. For political reformers, standardised civil service positions were the essence of good government. Jobs provided an identify to immigrants and recently-urbanised farm workers. They provided a sense of security for individuals and an organising principle for society.

Jobs functioned in so many ways that it is surprising how many organisations are now opting for other ways to define and manage work. The second job shift is underway. Its emergence can be seen in the increasing use of temporary and part-time workers and contracted-out services, the changing relationships between workers and management, the growing popularity of self-employment and small business. Indeed, 'de-jobbing' is proceeding at such a pace that many economists, management experts and futurists are now talking freely about the end of the job. Bridges predicts that the job as we now know it will disappear entirely—replaced by new kinds of flexible work assignments in post-job organisations—and be remembered only as a quaint artifact of the industrial age.

One reason for the change in work is the economic rules of the survival game among organisations that employ workers. To stay successful in today's hi-tech consumer economy, businesses have had to re-model themselves into what some experts call 'agile companies'—once that are able to respond quickly to conditions in ever-changing, fragmenting, competitive markets.

The 'knowledge worker', whose work involves not simply doing something, but also applying theoretical or analytical skills. Such workers are replacing the industrial labourer as the dominant part of the workforce—and their productive activities are likely to be organised and structured much differently from those of their assembly-line predecessors.

De-jobbing as a result of new technology or the emergence of a service economy is a phenomenon that gets a lot of attention these days; but it is not the whole story. At all levels of society, people are improvising livelihoods that do not fit the industrial-era model. Immigrants to the developed countries, often unable to find steady jobs, nevertheless find places in the new landscape by being mobile, flexible, resourceful and imaginative: they moonlight, work part-time, share jobs, start small businesses. Their lives are often extremely difficult, but they are also instructive to those of us who believe you either have a job or you're out of luck.

It is too early to evaluate the implications of this multifaceted transformation of work, or to dismiss it as simply good or bad. Nevertheless, one cannot deny that it is taking place, and will bring about dramatic social changes.

On the downside, the job shift is causing great hardships for many workers and their families. It poses serious challenges to policy-makers, political activists and labour leaders. The basic question appears to be whether the key to global employment-development strategy is to play 'catch-up'—trying to bring millions of people around the world into jobs in industries and the public sector; or to play 'leapfrog'—creating new forms of employment.

The proposal to generate more employment in agriculture, for example, is based on new demand for agricultural exports from developing countries. The policies designed to make the most of this opportunity include measures to upgrade technology, raise productivity, ensure the supply of essential inputs, establish marketing and distribution channels, create links between agriculture and industry, and cater to export markets.

The issue of part-time work, another kind of employment that is seriously undervalued in the traditional industrial-era job mind-set. Part-time work may not offer much at this point to developing countries, where many people are under employed and wages are low, but it can be of great help in more advanced economies. And it is likely to be a big part of the global work picture in the years ahead.

A certain agility may also be necessary in agriculture, particularly in countries that for many years have depended heavily on producing commodities such as sugar for export as a means of generating income and employment. As Northern laboratories develop non-agricultural substitutes for many of these commodities-and this is already beginning to happen—the bottom may fall out of 'monoculture' economies, only economic, but will have long-run political implications as communities attempt to reorganise themselves in response to the changed conditions. It is, therefore, in the interest of raw materials exporters to closely monitor current trends in biotechnology and the use of genetic resources and modify their internal policies in anticipation of potential long-term effects."

This calls for flexibility, and an ability to get information and to act on it. Government officials, development workers, community leaders and individuals will, in some respects, all have to be 'knowledge workers' if they are to keep ahead of global changes. Jobs are going to be created not just by putting people to work, but by finding—or creating—new niches where they can be productive.

It is still possible to talk about jobs for all, and to resist the assumption made by many economists that high levels of unemployment are now inevitable. But, as we move ahead into the global information economy, we may be moving back into an older conception of the job, and seeing it again as something you do, rather than as something you have—or that has you.

16

Towards Healthy Cities

More than a third of the urban population in developing world live in housing of such poor quality with such inadequate provision for water, sanitation, drainage, garbage collection and health care that their health is constantly under threat. But, properly planned, cities can be safe and healthy.

In the cities of India, it is common for one child in three to die before the age of five and for virtually all infants, children and adults who survive to have disease burdens many times higher than they should.

Diarrhoea, tuberculosis and respiratory infections (each among the largest causes of death) are generally much increased by over-crowding. Many accidental injuries happen when there are three or more persons living in each small room in shelters made of flammable materials and there is little chance of providing occupants (especially children) with protection from open fires or stoves.

But cities also include some of the India's safest and most healthy neighbourhoods. High densities allow much lower costs for supplying each household with piped, treated water supplies and most forms of health, educational and emergency services.

Sanitation and drainage may be costly in cities, as complex systems are needed to cope with high densities and large population concentrations but city households can generally afford to pay more—and are prepared to do so if they get a good service.

Cities may be considered ecologically unsustainable because of high consumption and waste levels but well planned and managed cities can combine high living standards with remarkably low levels of energy consumption, resource use and wastes. The concentration of people and production creates many more possibilities of collecting and recycling wastes and for walking, bicycling and a high quality public transport.

For many, city-life is one of excessive work loads and drudgery, yet cities remain centres of culture—including the visual and decorative arts, music, dance, theatre and literature. Most cities have a large reserve of young people on whose initiative and energy they could draw to improve conditions—yet most such people find that their cities offer them little hope and little prospect of employment. If cities have such potential to provide healthy, stimulating and valued places to live and work for all age groups, why do so few achieve this?

Supporting Change

Much of the explanation is the lack of 'good governance'. Good governance in any city means encouragement and support from all levels of government for a greater range of investments of capital, expertise and time by individuals, households, communities, voluntary organisations and NGOs—as well as private enterprises. In most cities in India, the total value of investments made by people in their own homes and neighbourhoods exceeds many times the total value of capital investments made by city and municipal authorities. Yet governments and aid agencies usually ignore (or deem illegal) most such efforts.

Most households who want their own home cannot afford to purchase one—or at least one that is legal. They cannot obtain housing loans so the cost of the house purchase can be spread over a number of years—as they cannot meet the (usually) inappropriate conditions set by banks or housing finance institutions. If they turn to building their own home—as most do—they have to occupy or purchase the site illegally. They often have to build on dangerous sites—in floodplains or on slopes with frequent landslides or mudslides—as the cost of safer sites is too high.

Even if they can qualify, for a housing loan, most such loans are for finished houses, not for incremental construction. And even when they have developed their own home and neighbourhood into a viable residential area, governments usually refuse to provide these with roads, water supplies, drains and other essential infrastructure, because they are 'illegal'.

What would cities look like today if governments had supported these individuals and community efforts by ensuring that land, building materials, credit and technical advice were as cheap and readily available as possible? Or if government-community partnerships had been formed to, at least, improve water supply, sanitation, drainage and health care.

These works within what is often called the 'social economy'—the great variety of initiatives and actions that are organised and controlled locally and that are not profit-oriented. The social economy, includes the work of citizen groups, residents' associations, street or barrio clubs, youth clubs, and parent associations that support local schools. It includes many voluntary groups that provide services for the elderly, the physically disabled or other individuals in need of social. It often includes many initiatives that make cities safer and more fun-helping provide supervised play space, sport and recreational opportunities for children and youth. It may provide formal or informal supervision or maintenance of parks, squares and other public spaces.

The social economy not only 'gets things done' but also creates a dense fabric of relationships that allows citizens to work together in identifying and acting on local problems. Its value to a 'healthy city' is enormous, even if it is often forgotten by governments and international agencies.

The capacity of city authorities to govern is not the same as the capacity to invest, since these authorities can do much to encourage and support the social economy. City authorities can often greatly increase the supply and reduce the cost of land for housing by changing inappropriate regulations, streamlining planning and land use control procedures and making better use of publicly owned land.

City authorities should also have the main role in enforcing legislation on, air and water pollution and occupational health and safety. This does not require large investments by public authorities, but it can do much to improve health and the quality of life in a city. Good governance also means managing competing claims and finding common ground between enterprises, trade unions and residents about what should be done to make the city more healthy.

Achieving a healthy city needs a representative political system through which the priorities of citizens and businesses can influence policies and actions. Democratic structures remain among the best checks on the misallocation of resources by city and municipal governments. Actively involving a wide range of local groups in developing 'city governance' helps ensure that the different priorities of a wide range of groups are addressed.

The key issue is not so much identifying what should be done to achieve more healthy cities. This is well known. It is identifying how it should be done, especially how governments and international agencies can support a vast range of activities by individuals, households and communities that help build and maintain healthy cities—which to date they have ignored or even (for many governments) repressed.

17

Children's Health and the Environment

Children today live in an environment vastly different from that of a few generations ago. Economic development, increased urbanisation and the consequences of war in many countries have added to the traditional environmental hazards, those problems associated with environmental pollution. Thus, while some traditional children's diseases such as diarrhoea, malnutrition and infectious diseases persist in many countries, environmentally-related illness such as asthma, respiratory illnesses due to Environmental Tobacco Smoke (ETS), as well as mortality and morbidity due to injuries, are increasing. In childhood cancer in some countries and the potential risks of endocrine-disrupting chemicals are among the emerging health threats that need careful vigilance. Children of lower socio-economic status are likely to suffer disproportionately from all these health threats as a consequence of living in highly polluted environments, poor quality housing, lower levels of education, and of restricted access to environmental and health care services.

Children's Vulnerability

The concern for children's vulnerability to

environmental health threats is based on several factors. Children receive greater exposure than adults do because they drink more water, eat more food and have higher breathing rates per unit of body weight. Because they are undergoing rapid growth and development, toxicant effects at specific times may have irreversible consequences. For example, if vital connections between nerve cells fail to form during brain development, there is high risk that the resulting neuro-behavioural dysfunction will be permanent and irreversible. Also, because most children have more future years of life than adults, they have more time to develop any chronic disease that may be triggered by early environmental exposures.

Public Health Threats

Asthma, injuries, and the effects of Environmental Tobacco Smoke (ETS) are among the most significant public health threats to children. Childhood asthma is increasingly prevalent in all most all countries. What causes asthma is not known, but several environmental factors, such as indoor air quality (particularly exposure to the house-dust mite) and ETS, have bee linked with the increase in asthma. In addition, outdoor air pollutants such as particulates, sulphur dioxide and ozone can exacerbate asthma symptoms. ETS, especially smoking by the mother, is a known risk factor for asthma. ETS is also known to cause acute and chronic middle ear disease and is associated with Sudden Infant Death Syndrome (SIDS).

Potential for Prevention

The variation in asthma and injury rates and the evidence of the role of certain environmental factors underline the potential for prevention. Public policies should seek to avoid preventable childhood diseases by preventing exposures to environmental agents and considering children's characteristics and susceptibilities in the development of environmental health legislation. Promoting citizen awareness and participation in policy-making through education and access to environmental information are important elements in achieving a safe environment for children. In this context, children are not only consumers with rights, but also citizens who can play an active role towards their own protection.

International Awareness

Several international agreements have acknowledged children's vulnerabilities and have committed their signatories to protect children's health from the effects of a deteriorating environment. This year, many countries will address several of the environmental health threats to children through international and national action. It is expected that a large international collaborative initiative will result under the guidance of WHO and other international organisations.

18

The Environment, the Economy and Public Health—An Integrated View

The environment is central to the health of people and their economies. Just as a foetus is totally dependent on the life-support system of the mother during her pregnancy, so the health and vitality of people and their economies are totally dependent on their environments. Unfortunately, many people do not see it that way. They either see the environment as dependent on the economy—such as the politician who says: "let's make the economy strong, then we'll fix the environment when we can afford it"—or they see little connection between health and the environment, whether they are 'deep greens' campaigning on ecological issues or doctors treating individual patients and individual illnesses. Whether we are politicians, greens or doctors, is there not a more efficient way to fulfil our aims? For this, a broader perspective is essential.

All economies are sub-systems of the larger environmental system which provides the:

- sources of energy and materials;
- sinks for pollution and other wastes;

- ❒ services of water, nutrients and carbon recycling;
- ❒ space for living, working and aesthetics ("a walk in the woods and the song of a bird").

Neglect of this life-support system of the '4 S's' leads to weaker or defunct economies as vegetation, food, soils, water or air become contaminated or exhausted and gradually fail to support economic activity. This is dramatically illustrated in the Aral Sea region, or the collapsed Canadian salmon fishing communities.

Indirect Social Costs

Less catastrophic but still costly is where economic damage is caused by pesticides and nutrient contamination of groundwater, involving millions of rupees in water treatment. This is a social cost to the economy that the agricultural sector does not include in the price of its food: an economic distortion that reduces the real wealth of society via false price signals that encourage the over-use of pesticides and fertilisers. Similarly, the 'external' costs on society of road-respiratory-induced accidents, noise, respiratory and circulatory diseases and congestion amount to a lot of money to any government but these costs are not borne by transport users, which mean that transport is encouraged beyond the level that is economic for society as a whole. By internalising these externalities via taxes and other means, the market prices for transport would become fairer and more efficient. Currently only about 30 per cent of transport externalities are covered by transport taxes. But if the health of an economy is dependent on the health of its environment, what about the health of its people?

Without access to the basics of clean water, shelter, fresh air and food, people obviously suffer. Even in more developed economies where the link between everyday life and the environment is not so visible, the role of environmental factors in disease and well-being is significant. Most of the major diseases such as heart disease, cancer, respiratory diseases and allergies have an environmental as well as a genetic component within a multi-factorial chain of causation. And while each environmental factor may be small, if the links in the chain of causation are inter-dependent, as they often appear to be then removing even a small link can break the chain.

Environmental Factors

Take asthma in children, for example. There seem to be many causes, from a child's genetic inheritance to its nutritional status, which in turn help determine how it reacts to the many environmental factors, both indoor (such as mites, pets, damp, environmental tobacco smoke, nitrogen oxides) and outdoor (such as pollen and pollution from industry and traffic), that have been implicated in asthma causation. Therefore it is clear that diagnoses of asthma and many other diseases should systematically embrace environmental factors. This will be a significant challenge for doctors whose time is scarce and whose training is not usually appropriate.

This multi-causal chain will vary in its exact make-up from child to child, but for children overall, even if the environmental factors such as damp housing or traffic fumes may be less important than, say, genetic make-up or nutritional status, the environmental factors may be the once that can be most cost effectively removed, thus breaking the casual chain. And, as with many environmental issues, there are secondary benefits of action, such as less noise or fewer accidents from traffic reduction, or energy savings from dry houses, which further justify the environmental actions even where exact causations are not well understood.

The environmental causes of disease and ill health are a controversial and ill understood area of science and opinions vary about their significance. Some say that, for Western Europe, perhaps 2-3 per cent of public disease and ill-health is determined by known environmental factors but others maintain that it must be far more significant. They point to the sharp increase over the last two or three decades in asthma, allergies, and cancers (particularly of the reproductive organs such as breast and testicles) and related ill-health such as sperm count decline, which cannot be explained by genetic causes. They also observe that the large differences in health between the socio-economic classes cannot be explained without involving significant environmental causation.

It is a thought that the ubiquitous presence of low doses of mixtures of chemicals in food, drink, air, consumer products and the general environment are playing some role in public ill health, even if the evidence for this is far from substantial.

Impact on Public Health

But what about environmental programmes and campaigns being little concerned with health? Well, history so far shows that the environment only gets serious attention when it is seen to be damaging either the economy or public health. Yet because 'everything connects' in 'socio-enviro' systems, actions to stop infectious diseases from water contamination, or to reduce skin cancer from ozone depletion, leads to a better environment for all species. And if upland forests are preserved because they are seen to be cheaper and more effective water regulators (which reduce the risk of lowland flooding) than dams, then upland biodiversity benefits anyway, even if it was last in the queue for political attention.

Although public health may be seen by some as only a small part of 'the environment', much environmental progress depends upon the political weight of the health impacts. For example, the cost benefit exercise on the current multi-pollutant/effect programme on acidification, eutrophication and low-level ozone shows that it is the benefits to human health, not eco-system damage, that provide the main economic justification for further reductions in SO_2, NO_x and NH_3. Ecologists need the language of public health in order to maximise political support for the environment. So, it is out of our specialist 'boxes' of economics, health and ecology, and into a shared systems approach, with integrated programmes that build partnerships for progress.

19

Action for Safe Motherhood

Countries vary enormously in terms of the situations and challenges they face and their capacity to address these. However, experience from around the world over the past decade has demonstrated that a number of features are common to successful efforts to address maternal mortality. Reducing maternal mortality requires coordinated, long-term efforts. Actions are needed within families and communities, in society as a whole, in health systems, and at the level of national legislation and policy. Further, interactions among the interventions in these areas are critical to reducing maternal mortality and to building and supporting momentum for change.

Legislative and Policy Actions

Changes in legislation and policy are essential to ensure safe motherhood. Long-term political commitment is an essential prerequisite. When decision-makers at the highest levels are resolved to address maternal mortality, the resources needed will be mobilised and the essential policy decisions will be taken. Without this level of commitment over the long term, projects cannot become programmes and activities cannot be sustained.

A supportive social, economic, and legislative environment allows women to overcome the various obstacles that limit their access to health care, such as distance from their homes to appropriate health facilities, lack of transport and, more critically, financial and social barriers. Proper maternal health care is limited when women have to pay for services and essential drugs, and when they must bear substantial hidden costs such as time lost for housework, paid employment, food production, and child care. Legislation that supports women's access to care must be formulated to permit health workers at the periphery of the health system to perform specific life-saving functions. Failing this, only highly skilled health professionals, based largely in urban centres, can provide such care, and only women with sufficient money and the means to reach such centres can benefit from it.

With these objectives, careful review of national laws and policies is necessary, particularly in the following areas:

- ***Family planning:*** Statutes that restrict women's access to family planning services (*e.g.* by requiring that a woman be married or that she should have her husband's approval) should be repealed. Policies must ensure that all couples and individuals have access to good-quality, voluntary, client-oriented, and confidential family planning information and to services that offer a wide choice of effective contraceptive methods. Policies should address regulatory, social, economic, and cultural factors that limit women's control over sexuality and reproduction, in order that pregnancies that are too early, too late, or too frequent may be avoided.
- ***Adolescents and children:*** Policies and programmes should encourage later marriage and

childbearing and an expansion of the economic and educational opportunities for girls and women. Promotion of good nutrition in childhood and adolescence, as well as supplementation if necessary during pregnancy, provides protection for both women and their future children. Policies should also enable adolescents to take responsibility for and protect their sexual and reproductive health, and facilitate their access to health information and services. All children, before they reach the age at which they become sexually active, need to be taught the risks of unprotected sex and helped to develop the skills needed to protect themselves from sexual coercion.

- ***Barriers to access:*** Assigning health workers trained in midwifery to village-based health facilities can help overcome problems of distance and transport. Health workers should also be trained to deal sympathetically with women patients. Policies should support the provision of services at minimum cost; at the same time, health workers should have job security, be paid adequate wages, and be provided with sufficient supplies to do their jobs. Policies that will increase women's decision-making power, particularly in regard to their own health, are also essential.

- ***Regulation of practice:*** Protocols and statutes aimed at providing both routine maternal care and referral facilities for obstetric complications at each level of the health system need to be developed. Responsibilities at each level for supervision, deployment of health care personnel, remuneration, and reporting procedures must be defined nationally. Development and promotion of education and training curricula are important, as is the setting of national norms and standards to govern the selection of trainees, trainers, and supervisors.

- ***Delegation of authority:*** Services should be decentralised so that facilities are available as close to people's homes as possible. Adequate supplies and equipment and trained staff should be available in all health facilities, particularly in rural and remote areas, together with written policies and protocols to guide service provision and to allow certain functions to be delegated to personnel at lower levels (when appropriately trained).

- ***Abortion:*** Availability of services for management of abortion complications and post-abortion care should be ensured by appropriate legislation. Where abortion is not prohibited by law, facilities for the safe termination of pregnancy should be made available. National policy can discourage unsafe abortion practices by promoting protection against unwanted pregnancy, and national health campaigns to publicize the risks of unsafe abortion and the need to recognise and seek treatment for abortion complications.

20

Safe Motherhood is a Human Rights Issue

The death of a woman during pregnancy or childbirth is not only a health issue but also a matter of social injustice. Of the human rights currently acknowledged in national constitutions and in regional and international human rights treaties, many can be applied to safe motherhood. Many such treaties and conventions are based on the 1948 Declaration of Human Rights *(i)* they include the Convention on the Elimination of All Forms of Discrimination against Women, *(ii)* the Convention on the Rights of the Child, *(iii)* the European Convention for the Protection of Human Rights and Fundamental Freedoms, *(iv)* the American Convention on Human Rights, *(v)* and the African Charter on Human and Peoples' Rights.

Human rights of relevance to safe motherhood can be grouped into the following four principal categories:

- *Rights relating to life, liberty and security of the person*, which require governments to ensure both access to appropriate health care during pregnancy and childbirth, and women's rights to decide whether, when, and how often to bear children. Governments must therefore address factors within the economic, legal, social, and health systems that deny women these fundamental rights.

- *Rights relating to the foundation of families and of family life*, which require governments to provide access to health services and other facilities that women need to establish families and to enjoy life within a family.

- *Rights relating to health care and the benefits of scientific progress, including health information and education*, which require governments to provide access to good sexual and reproductive health care with appropriate referral systems. The measures needed to ensure safe motherhood can be provided through primary health care irrespective of a country's level of economic development. Central to these rights is information on a range of reproductive health issues, including family planning, abortion, and sex education.

- *Rights relating to equality and nondiscrimination*, which require governments to provide access to services such as education and health care without discriminatory ground such as sex, marital status, age, and socio-economic class. Discriminatory policies include requirements for a woman to obtain the consent of her husband for particular health care interventions, requirements for parental authorisation which have a differential impact on girls, and laws that criminalise medical procedures that only women need. Governments are in violation of their obligations when they fail to implement laws that effectively protect women's interests or to allocate health resources to meet women's particular need for safe pregnancy and childbirth.

The actions that governments need to take to promote safe motherhood as a human right fall into three groups:

- *Reform of laws* that prevent women from attaining the highest possible levels of health and nutrition needed for safe pregnancy and childbirth and that inhibit access to reproductive health information and services such as laws requiring women in need of health care to seek the authorisation of husband or other family members first.
- *Implementation of laws* that foster women's right to good health and nutrition and that protect women's health interests such as laws that prohibit child marriage, female genital mutilation, rape, and sexual abuse. Every effort should be made to implement laws that encourage the healthy timing of births, such as those that support the education of girls, set a minimum age for marriage, and ensure women's access to essential health care.
- *Application of human rights* in national legislation and policy to advance safe motherhood.

21

What is Known About Reducing Maternal Mortality?

Historical records demonstrate the significant improvements that can be achieved when key interventions are in place. Reductions in maternal mortality took place in Sweden during the 1800s, for example, as a result of a national policy favouring professional midwifery care for all births, coupled with establishment of standards for quality of care. By the beginning of the 20th century, maternal mortality in Sweden was the lowest around 230 per 1,00,000 live births compared with over 500 per 1,00,000 in the mid-1880s. In Denmark, Japan, Netherlands, and Norway, similar strategies produced comparable results. In England and Wales, significant reductions in maternal mortality were not apparent until the 1930s; at the national level, political commitment to the strategy was achieved only slowly and the introduction of professional midwifery was correspondingly delayed. In every case, however, the key to these improvements was the institution of fully professional maternity care.

In the USA, where strategy focused on hospital delivery by doctors, maternal mortality remained high because it proved difficult to establish adequate regulatory frameworks and mechanisms to ensure quality of care. In 1930, the maternal mortality ratio in the USA was still 700 per 1,00,000 live births compared with 430 in England and Wales.

More recently, India witnessed significant reductions in maternal mortality in a relatively short period. From a level of over 1500 per 1,00,000 live births in 1940-1945, maternal mortality fell to 555 per 1,00,000 in 1950-1955, 239 per 1,00,000 within 10 years, and 95 per 1,00,000 by 1980. The figure is now 30 per 1,00,000. These improvements followed the introduction of a system of health facilities around the country allied to an expansion of midwifery skills and the spread of family planning. During the 1950s most births in India took place at home with the assistance of untrained birth attendants. By the end of the 1980s over 85 per cent of all births were attended by trained personnel.

Similar evidence of the effectiveness of health care interventions is available from China, Cuba, and Malaysia. These countries established community-based maternal health care systems comprising prenatal, delivery, and postpartum care and a system of referral to a higher level of care in the event of obstetric complications.

What these examples clearly demonstrate is that a country's overall economic wealth is not in itself the most important determinant of maternal mortality. There are numerous other examples of countries with modest levels of GNP which have achieved low maternal mortality.

22

Why Don't We Stop Tuberculosis?

Tuberculosis, a disease many people associate with sequestered sanatoriums that were long ago abandoned or razed, has now reemerged as the number one killer among the infectious or communicable diseases. The current TB epidemic is expected to grow worse, especially in India, because of the evolution of multi-drug-resistant strains and the emergence of AIDS, which compromises human immune systems and makes them more susceptible to infectious diseases.

The resurgence of tuberculosis comes at a time when other infectious diseases that were once thought to be well-controlled—malaria and cholera, among them—have increased and new diseases, notably AIDS, have emerged. Despite the advances in modern medicine, infectious diseases have persisted and continue to have a major effect on public health; in the 50 years following the discovery of antibiotics, efforts to control age-old epidemics have been overcome not by a lack of medical knowledge but by structural problems, including the lack of adequate health care in many parts of India, and increased rates of travel and migration.

Tuberculosis has special characteristics that set it apart from other infectious diseases, most of which rely on mosquitoes, rats, or water to transmit infection. Tubercle bacilli only live in human tissues, and tuberculosis can only be transmitted by close contact with an infected person. In a healthy individual, the immune system is normally able to wall off and isolate the bacilli in a nodule. This essentially neutralises the tubercle bacillus, so the person has what is referred to as an inert infection. If the immune system remains strong, there is only a 5 to 10 per cent chance of developing TB from an inert infection. But if the immune system is under severe stress—from HIV, diabetes, or chemotherapy for cancer, for example—the chances that the infection will develop into disease increase to as much as 10 per cent in a single year.

A person who has active TB can spread the infection simply by coughing, sneezing, singing, or even talking. Another person has only to inhale the bacilli to become infected. If the infection is not detected and treated promptly, one person with active tuberculosis can infect an average of 10 to 14 people in one year and sometimes many more.

Inert TB infections may show no symptoms at all. Only if those infections are activated will these people be at risk of developing the disease and transmitting it to others. Unfortunately, little is known about what activates a latent TB infections beyond the fact that people with healthy immune systems run a low risk of developing an active case of TB.

Because the already poor and disenfranchised Indian population carry a disproportionate burden of tuberculosis, the disease has a certain stigma attached to it. But the unsanitary and crowded living conditions that are often connected to poverty do not cause TB to spread; they increase the chances that the infection will spread from person to person and the chances that a person's immune system may already be weak and therefore less able to fight the infection. Despite the misconceptions, tuberculosis is exacerbated only by the failure to detect and treat the infection properly and by close contact with infected individuals.

More than 95 per cent of TB cases reported in 1995 were in the developing world, as estimated two-thirds of them in Asia. India accounted for 2.1 million cases. India is with a disproportionate number of cases because AIDS is spreading quickly, health services are inadequate, and little money is available for treatment.

To identify and diagnose TB must be combined with sufficient infrastructure and resources, such as vaccines, medicines, trained health personnel, and clinics. As with other diseases, funding for research and prevention and treatment programmes is essential. Thanks to modern medicine, there is a low-cost, effective TB treatment with high cure rates among infected adults. But if patients don't take the drugs consistently or don't complete treatment, TB strains develop that are more resistant to medicine, and sometimes even untreatable. If this drug regimen were used throughout India. It would reduce the rate of transmission and cut the number of deaths by half over the next 10 years.

The growing TB epidemic is a classic case of a public health crisis in India that could be headed off easily and inexpensively. Its fate will largely depend on the willingness of government and public health officials to invest up front in prevention and early intervention. If we ignore the extraordinary opportunity that exists now to fight the epidemic, we will pay a high price in lives and extensive health care costs later.

23

AIDS and the Responsibility of the Media

HIV/AIDS is one of the most terrible diseases the world has ever known. Estimates are that 37 million people worldwide are already infected with the deadly virus which weakens the human immunity system and leaves the body unprotected for the onslaught of a host of other diseases. So far, there is no vaccine to shield people against, HIV and there is no effective cure for the disease. This means that people inevitably die once they have caught the virus although some ten years or more may pass before the actual outbreak of AIDS in its final stages. UN figures say that 23 million of HIV/AIDS infected people live in sub-Saharan Africa alone—and all of them are doomed to die a painful death. At least 4 million newly infected were added to that number every year. As a result of the epidemic, life expectancy on the continent, which had been climbing persistently during the first three decades of post-independence development, will drop by ten years and more in many countries, especially in Southern Africa. And it will be the young, economically active people—who are also the sexually most active ones—that will be prominent among the victims. AIDS thus is not only a humanitarian disaster, it is also threatening to become another source of economic retardation and backwardness.

Why then there is still so little attention paid to the looming crisis? Why are African leaders not getting together to discuss what needs to be done to control the situation? Why are they not using every means at their disposal to hammer the message home to their people: AIDS can be reigned in through more responsible behaviour and a change in sexual practices?

In Europe and America, when AIDS surfaced as a common threat in the late 1980s, every effort was made to alarm the public and especially the most vulnerable groups homosexuals, sex workers, people with frequently changing sex partners—about the dangers of unprotected sex. It was especially through the media that the almost everybody became aware of the AIDS menace. Prominent individuals—film stars, pop musicians, artists—who had been infected with AIDS outed themselves in the media and used their fame in anti-AIDS campaigns. Existing taboos on sexual practices were deliberately broken, and safer sex became a publicly debated issue. Much emphasis was placed on using condoms as a cheap and simple, but usually effective means to avoid infection. As a result of the public awareness campaigns and the continuous media coverage, new HIV infections in industrial countries returned to a relatively low level, and the disease today is considered to be under control, even though no medical cure has yet been found to treat AIDS patients.

While these successes were achieved in developed countries, the disease has been spreading with increasing speed in Africa and, lately, in Asia. Here, the society has reacted with far less openness to the challenges posed by AIDS. For a long time, political leaders and the media negated the menace in the erroneous belief that AIDS was mainly a disease of the decadent West. When they work up to fact that AIDS was a problem not only for homosexuals in Los Angeles, London, or Berlin but also for 'normal' hetero-sexual men and women in Uganda, South Africa or India, sexual taboos and religious inhibitions as well as social customs and attitudes proved powerful obstacles to launching publicity campaigns on the model of the Western countries.

As a result, there is still far too little information in developing on AIDS as a disease and what people can do to protect themselves against it. A recent study published by Johns Hopkins University in the United States, for instance, shows that only between 5 and 33 per cent of unmarried men are using condoms in sexual intercourse to avoid infection with AIDS. With women, condoms are even less known or popular than with men. The study says that the number of couples using condoms regularly is still very low worldwide. Instead of the 6 to 9 billion condoms used at present, 24 billion are required to control new infections. This is a question of money, because many of the people who ought to use condoms are among the poorest groups in breaking down barriers created out of prejudice and ingrained sexual behaviour.

Here, the media have a vital role to play. It is not enough to put up a few posters in town which warn against AIDS. The message has to be direct and concrete—Mechai in Thailand has shown how a witty and effective pro-condom campaign can be conducted even in a country with; a strong Buddhist tradition—and it should not shy away from breaking sexual taboos. Equally important: all media should be used—news papers, radio, TV, films, video—to carry the message. AIDS awareness should always be part of reproductive health information, and needed, both are part of the same coin: if more condoms are used to prevent unwanted pregnancies, a welcome side-effect will be a reduction in new HIV infections.

AIDS and the menace it poses to the survival of large parts of African and Asian populations is not a pleasant subject. But it will not go away by keeping silent about its threat. Political leaders and the media must make it a topic for urgent action. And the people must change their sexual habits and behaviour and opt for safer sex. Otherwise, the future of whole regions on this globe will be grim.

24

Controlling the Global Tobacco Epidemic Towards a Transnational Response

Recent trends in the globalisation of the tobacco industry are reflected in the shifting of the burden of tobacco-related disease and deaths towards developing countries. Tobacco companies have proved sufficiently powerful to thwart comprehensive control programmes in all but a handful of countries. What new strategies are needed to control the epidemic in developing regions?

One billion people smoke worldwide and around 3.5 million die from tobacco-related illnesses annually. By 2030, this figure will rise to ten million, with 70 per cent of deaths in lower and middle income countries (LMICs). Four companies now control 75 per cent of global cigarette sales, as sophisticated strategies for supply, production and sales have produced increasingly popular global brands.

The onward march of Marlboro man epitomises this globalisation, exploiting the opportunities presented by trade liberalisation, regional organisations and the communications revolution. Control efforts are undermined by the industry's success in developing favourable relationships with many governments, the magnitude of their foreign direct investments and the scale of advertising, marketing and sponsorship campaigns. In addition, large-scale cigarette smuggling, which comprises one-third of total exports, depletes tax revenues and further jeopardises public health.

A unique response by the World Health Organisation (WHO) reflects the scale of the challenge. WHO is negotiating its first public health treaty: the Framework Convention on Tobacco Control. To be effective, this potentially powerful instrument must be backed up by strengthened national policies set within the context of globalisation and based on an appreciation of transnational tobacco industry strategies. In support of this process, an international team based at the London School of Hygiene and Tropical Medicine carried out pilot studies in Thailand and Zimbabwe. These aimed to initiate the development of guidelines for tobacco policy research in LMICs, where resources and expertise are frequently lacking.

The political sensitivities surrounding tobacco control reflect the complex array of powerful vested interests involved. The case studies showed that political mapping and stakeholder analysis can make a valuable contribution to understanding the opportunities and constraints for national control policies in an era of globalisation. For example, they found that the 1992 Global Agreement on Tariffs and Trade (GATT) ruling that opened Thailand's previously closed cigarette market had contradictory results:

- Thailand is a key market for tobacco companies seeking expansion in Asia;
- The US Trade Representatives secured access to the Thai market through GATT's insistence on equal treatment of domestic and foreign cigarette manufactures, and imports escalated rapidly;

- The GATT ruling also upheld the right to protect public health, giving a major impetus to health activists pressing the Thai government for action;
- Subsequent comprehensive control legislation has stabilised smoking rates in Thailand.

Control policies of wealthier countries cannot simply be transplanted to poorer nations. Knowledge of the complex policy environments surrounding tobacco control in LMICs is limited and effective policies will require:

- detailed analysis of the particular political and economic contexts;
- multidisciplinary expertise from public health and social science;
- links between researchers, policymakers and activists;
- support for national research capacity through the development of clear guidelines for tobacco policy analysis and their application by national researchers.

Finally, the enforced opening of internal industry documents provides an important new resource. Access to the depositories in Minnesota, USA, and Guildford, UK, and via the internet offers a unique opportunity to understand the global strategies of the tobacco companies. Analysis of their contents has so far focused on the United States. There is an urgent need to extend this attention to industry activities within LMICs.

25

Taking Poverty to Heart

Non-Communicable Diseases and the Poor

Non-Communicable Diseases (NCDs) are the leading cause of death worldwide. Their emergence as the predominant health problem in wealthy countries accompanied economic development. As a result, NCDs are often referred to as 'diseases of affluence'. But is this a misleading term? It suggests that these are not major problems for the world's poor, which is quite simply wrong, as this article illustrates. Is it time to rethink policy on NCDs?

NCDs include Cardiovascular Disease (CVD), such as stroke and heart attack, diabetes, chronic lung disease, cancer, diseases of bones and joints, and mental illness. The single biggest killer is coronary heart disease, followed by other CVDs, cancer and chronic lung disease. Diabetes is a major contributor to deaths from CVD, but also causes its own unique complications. Common risk factors for these conditions include smoking, physical activity, obesity and diets high in saturated fat and sodium and low in fruit and vegetables.

By 2020, NCDs will be the biggest cause of death in all regions apart from sub-Saharan Africa. It is predicted that in 2010, the number of people with diabetes worldwide will be double the level in 1995 and that the biggest increase (both proportionately and in absolute number) will be in poorer regions. CVD occurs at an earlier age in developing countries, increasing the potential adverse economic and social consequences.

NCDs are already major health problems for adults in the poorest countries of the world. Demographic data show that age-specific death rates from NCDs in Tanzania are higher than in wealthier countries. Mortality rates for some NCDs, such as stroke, are particularly high. However, while NCDs account for 80 per cent of adult deaths in developed regions the figure is less than 30 per cent in Tanzania, reflecting the continuing burden of infectious disease. Countries like Tanzania suffer the 'worst of both worlds'. Even within a country, 'diseases of affluence' is a misleading term. A more accurate label is 'diseases of Urbanisation'. Several studies from developing countries show increased levels of high blood pressure and other NCD risk factors in urban compared to rural populations. Even within urban areas, the more affluent do not always suffer the greatest burden.

The rise of NCDs in developing countries in inextricably linked to economic and cultural globalisation. This is exemplified by the activities of multinational tobacco companies. Tobacco-related deaths will exceed the toll due to HIV and become the single largest preventable cause of death by 2020. Curbing the effects of globalisation on the prevention and treatment of NCDs will also require regulation of food and agriculture multinationals and the pharmaceutical and healthcare industries.

Much of the projected rise in NCDs is preventable, particularly that due to smoking, poor diet, physical inactivity and obesity. Early action in some populations could prevent the emergence of these risk factors altogether; in other, the challenge is to reduce established levels. Although it is unclear whether all major risk factors are equally important in every region, the strength and consistency of data on the core risk factors in several ethnic groups justify preventative action now.

Lessons from risk factor intervention studies in rich and middle income countries suggest that success requires:

- broad intersectoral action
- community participation
- appropriate legislation
- involvement of appropriate NGOs
- health services changes—to manage those at high risk and promote public education.

Even apparently minor changes, such as a small fall in average population blood pressure, can have substantial benefits. However, some preventative programmes have produced disappointing results and almost all have failed to halt the ubiquitous increase in obesity. This highlights the difficulty of promoting healthy behaviour by individuals who are surrounded by barriers to change and inducements to lead an unhealthy lifestyle.

Health systems in developing countries face both a growing need for prevention programmes and increasing numbers of individuals requiring treatment. The complications of high blood pressure and diabetes can be reduced by the delivery of effective healthcare. Crucially, this entails:

- partnership between patients and health professionals with the knowledge, ability and resources to take appropriate measures over many years;

- cheap and effective drugs and the implementation of simple treatment protocols, as promoted by WHO and the CVD initiative of the Global Forum for Health Research.

An appropriate policy and strategic framework is essential for such initiatives to be effective on a large scale. Even in the poorest countries people are already seeking healthcare for NCDs in both the public and private sectors, particularly in urban areas. Whatever the balance of priorities between different conditions, existing resources should be used as effectively as possible, Rapid evaluation methods can provide policy-makers with information on the current levels and quality of care and identify the main opportunities for improving health services.

The proper planning and co-ordination of NCD prevention and treatment, whether globally or nationally, requires up-to-date data on risk factor and disease levels—currently missing for much of the world. To address this lack, the WHO Non-Communicable Disease and Mental Health Surveillance section is promoting a standardised approach to enable comparisons across regions and over time, preparing the first ever 'world risk status' report for the major NCDs. This will provide a truly global perspective on the size and nature of the problem.

As this article has shown, NCDs are major health problems even in the world's poorest countries, including those regions where infectious diseases continue to take a huge toll. The NCD burden will grown substantially in low land middle-income countries over the next 10 to 20 years. NCDs will increasingly demand attention and require the right balance between competing priorities for prevention, cure and care. In meeting this challenge, national policy-makers will need to follow the lead of WHO and develop a strategic framework that plans for surveillance, prevention and appropriate health sector reforms.

26

Health Care Relief in Conflict Situations

What Can we Learn From the Food Relief Experience?

Conflicts and war occur in many of the poorest nations where populations already suffer from severe ill-health. War leads to an increase in disease and to a worsening of the already fragile condition of populations. Health care itself becomes a victim of conflict. Many deaths which occur during these emergencies are not discretely related to the conflict itself but are the result of lacking access to public health services. Furthermore, conflict itself but are the result of lacking access to public health services. Furthermore, conflict contributes to the deterioration of already pre-existing structural weaknesses of the health care system. An example is the period of internal conflict in Uganda (1970-1986) when health services declined in the aftermath of the war due to the impact of foreign assistance and the planning vacuum in which the activities took place.

The Impact of Conflict on Health Care

Conflict and civil strife may lead to a major disruption of health services. This is not only a result of physical destruction but also of finding shortages since national governments increase spending on military activities. Casualties increase the demand for curative services which can divert already limited resources from preventive care.

In the case of the Sudanese civil war a large majority of health professionals was forced to abandon rural health services and left for urban areas or neighbouring countries in order to find new employment. Entire preventive health services such as immunization as well as water and sanitation projects collapsed leaving the population exposed to infectious diseases and epidemics. In urban areas, the gap in public health care provision in sometimes filled with the expansion of private services. In rural areas, private sector involvement in health care is rather marginal, apart from some omission hospitals or pharmacies. Therefore the non-formal health care sector often makes a substantial contribution towards health care.

With the rise of internal conflicts in Africa, more people suffer from emergency situations. This also increases the influence and impact of international donors External assistance nowadays accounts for more than 25 per cent of government health expenditure in sub-Saharan Africa.

The size of donor involvement reflects the power of international agencies to control the policy domaine. Countries in conflict or post-conflict situations are under pressure to 'rescue' their health systems and accept global policies in exchange for aid assistance and relief.

However, in the period after 1991, donor organisations tended to increase their expenditures for high profile humanitarian operations rather than ordinary development activities. This shift may reflect the increasing influence of media covering some of the conflicts. Too often, organisations intervene with ad-hoc assistance without sufficient consultation at local level.

Donors' Perceptions in Designing Relief Interventions

Today, in many parts of sub-Saharan Africa development assistance has virtually collapsed and has been substituted by relief assistance. The problem is that relief interventions are based on a Western construction of reality, reflecting what is desirable and necessary in times of conflict. Most interventions therefore stress physical and material needs, presuming that the social aspect of food and health is not an immediate issue to address.

The question which arises here is on who's views and perceptions these needs are based? While donors interests may be guided from the perspective of ill-health, the recipient government may be concerned with the collapse of the economy. However, any intervention needs to take into account that local knowledge and practices are shaped by state interests as well as power relationships. The common belief that health care systems always collapse due to conflict is sometimes mistaken, considering the fact that today's internal conflicts are often fragmented, conflicts do not necessarily result in a breakdown of the health care delivery system.

Donors tend to respond with a 'package' approach and developing countries ministries of health increasingly play a symbolic role. The evidence suggests that international organisations tend to create verticle programmes which undermine national public health programmes. Foreign interventions are technically sophisticated and reorienting health are towards a more curative approach. Too little attentions given to strengthen the health care system within its own limits, providing more appropriate technology, drugs and emphasizing the training of local health staff.

Another vital issue concerns the existence of already fragile health information systems. Agencies tend to bring their own systems which leads to further fragmentation. The local perspective on what are the 'basic needs' in physical and social health are usually not considered. Health relief interventions do not recognise the potential of the communities and the non-formal health sector such as healers and traditional midwifes in supporting and maintaining health care sector presents a substantial contribution towards health. It is not the question between choosing either allopathic or traditional services, it is more the decision which kind of illness will be best treated by which practitioner. There is a need in further exploring the role of this sector particularly since this is sometimes the only service available for certain populations.

Responding to Local Needs

More community-based public health interventions could be vital to reduce mortality and morbidity. For example in Somalia during the 1992 war and famine high mortality rates due to measles and diarrhoea could have been prevented by involving the communities in primary health care activities such as immunization and nutrition improvement.

In the African context Tigray is an example where health services had been sustained and partially expanded during the civil war against the Ethiopian government. Local government structures called baitos promoting social and economic development. Baitos encouraged communities to establish revolving funds for drugs and medical equipment. It actually functioned as an early type of community financing system.

As mentioned above, the challenge in changing health care relief strategies is to overcome the approach of short-term interventions, particularly in a changing conflict environment where conflicts are complex and interruptions are no longer short-term. Therefore interventions need to be linked with the process of conflict resolution to avoid health care or food aid being used by politically dominant groups.

Food Relief in Conflict Situations

Food interventions have both a survival and a production function. For example, food-for-work may be part of an income programme or food aid can be monetised to generate local currency. However, food aids has to be seen beyond the objective to fulfil nutritional goals, it also defines relationships between social groups in regard to food accessibility and how food is shared. Food aid is aiming to meet people's basic food requirements and minimising risk and severity of disease by complementing services such as basic health care.

In more stable political conditions where free food aid is given it presents an income transfer by releasing income which normally is spent on food. However, in conflict situations food relief frequently becomes part of the dynamics of conflict such in the case of Sudan where it is used to sustain the struggle between the North and the South without resolving it. Furthermore, the military attack food supplies in the fight against rebels who depend on the support from the communities.

Health is also a matter of food security. When food insecurity coincides with conflict situations, health and survival are threatened. Food security provides some concepts on how and why vulnerable households manage to survive in periods of hardship (coping strategies).

Coping Strategies in African Trouble Zones

Today, most conflicts in Africa such as the ones in the Great Lake Region, Angola or Congo cause major problems of food insecurity. They are linked to the civil wars which produce substantial social disruption as a result of massive population movements. The analysis of coping strategies showed that household respond to these conflict situations by eating less, selling livestock and land, or trying to find new sources of income.

In some emergency situations, however, such coping mechanisms may fail. In the case of the war in Mozambique food aid was vital since coping strategies were limited and people had to sell all their assets which was particular true for internationally displaced persons and refugees.

It has been argued that food relief bypasses local structures in favour of those qualifying on a nutrition status criterion, decided by international organisations, or it may attract populations to refugee camps to receive free food rations and thereby undermines local production. In the case of Rwanda food aid was targeted at the internally displaced and left out the local population. This can be due to donor bias in needs assessment.

Food scarcity is not always so result of civil war but its creation may be rather a political objective. An example is food relief manipulated by local elites and the military like in the case of Sudan. It can be summarised that generally relief operations often bear the risk of fueling the process of instability and violence rather than helping to contain the situation.

Lessons from Food Relief for the Health Sector?

Through the experience of food relief in recent civil wars such as Sudan, Somalia, Mozambique etc., there has been an increasing awareness of the economic and political context in which operations takes place. Like food relief, health care is a political tool which can, if not properly targeted, undermine peoples access to health care services. While food production is linked to food security, it is more difficult to identify factors leading to self-sufficiency in health care.

As mentioned above, food aid is aiming to insure survival. It also has an economic aspect, protecting household assets. Health care relief is targeted to assure immediate physical survival based on the importance of social health. Unfortunately, curative interventions hardly consider the socio-cultural dimension of health. Therefore it would be beneficial if health care interventions consider local norms and traditions. Interventions should be compatible an complement local health programmes. The emphasis should be on strengthening formal and non-formal health institutions both in service provision and training.

In food relief, distribution and needs assessment identification are controversial issues for discussion. While the programme design is shaped by donors perceptions, the actual programmes are influenced by the priorities of some powerful leaders as well as the socio-economic and political context.

Health care interventions need to analyse these issues in the context of economic and political systems in order to identify the most vulnerable groups, for example populations living in areas which are more, operations require a stronger involvement of communities both as users and active participants to carry out and maintain public health programmes.

There is a need for a new concept to be designed which applied to chronic emergencies. In the absence of a policy framework, guidelines need to be developed in order to overcome the inconsistency in planning and implementation. Donors need to change their assumptions on which they plan their health relief responses. A starting point in improving the efficiency of these operations is to provide institutional support to local authorities and organisations and involve them in the planning and implementation of programmes.

27

Stop Child Labour

Although the internationally recommended minimum age for work is 15 years and the number of child workers under the age of 10 is far from negligible, almost all the data available on child labour concerns the 10-to-14 age group.

Traditionally, the proportion of working children has been much higher in rural than in urban areas—nine out of ten are engaged in agricultural or related activities. In the towns and cities of India where child labour has increased steadily as a result of the rapid urbanisation of recent years, working children are found mainly in trade and services and to a lesser extent in the manufacturing section.

Available statistics suggest that more boys than girls work. It should be borne in mind, however, that the number of working girls is often under estimated by statistical surveys, as they usually do not take into account full-time housework performed by many children, the vast majority of whom are girls, in order to enable their parents to go to work.

Girls, moreover, tend to work longer hours, on average, than do boys. This is especially, true for the many girls employed as domestic workers, a type of employment in which hours of work are typically extremely long. This is also the case of girls employed in other types of jobs who, in addition to their professional activity, must help with the housework in their parents' home.

One of the factors affecting the supply of child labour is the high cost, in real terms, of obtaining an education. Many children work to cover the costs of school expenses. But many schools serving the poor are of such abysmal quality or chances of upward mobility for graduates are so slim, that the expected return is not equal to the sacrifice made . . . . While it is true that many children drop out of school because they have to work, it is equally true that many become so discouraged by school that they prefer to work.

In manufacturing industries, children are most likely to be employed when their labour is less expensive or less troublesome than that of adults, when other labour is scarce, and when they are considered irreplaceable by reason of their size or perceived dexterity.

Many working children face significant threats to their health and safety. The majority are involved in farming and are routinely exposed to harsh climate, sharpened tools, heavy loads as well, increasingly, as to toxic chemicals and motorised equipment. Others, particularly girls working as domestic servants away from their homes, are frequent victims of physical, mental and sexual abuses which can have devastating consequences on their health.

Prostitution is another type of activity in which children, especially girls, are increasingly found. The AIDS epidemic is a contributing factor to this trend, as adults see the use of children for sexual purposes as the best means of preventing infection. The laissez-faire attitude of the authorities incharge of national and international tourism is also largely responsible for the current situation.

Another extremely serious problem is child slavery in India. A large number of child slaves are to be found in agriculture, domestic help, the sex, industry, the carpet and textile industries, quarrying and brickmaking." Child slavery predominates mainly where there are social systems based on the exploitation of poverty, such as debt bondage, when the motivation is the debt incurred by a family to meet a social or religious obligation or simply to acquire the means of survival.

There is a growing body of opinion that national and international efforts need to be more sharply focused on the most abusive and hazardous forms of child labour, granting them first concern and priority. Perhaps the most telling social argument against child labour is that its effects are highly discriminatory, adding to the burden and disadvantage of individuals and groups already among the socially excluded while benefiting those who are privileged. For that reason, child labour is inconsistent with democracy and social justice.

Action Required at the National Level

In the majority of states of India where child labour is common, the action taken until now to combat it has in no way been proportional to the extent and gravity of the problem. Many state governments have left it to economic growth and legislation alone to provide the solution. Experience has shown however that, unless specific measures are taken, growth in itself rarely benefits the very poor and that legislation means little where it is not vigorously enforced.

The problem of child labour will not be solved overnight. It is one of the many facets of poverty and underdevelopment. Resources available to reduce its extent and damaging effects are by definition scarcest in India that need them the most. Priorities must therefore be set.

No Effective Programmes Without Hard Information

Research: Almost everywhere, hard information is lacking on how many children are working, what they are doing, where and in what conditions. Without such data, it is virtually impossible to develop effective policies and programmes. Establishing, in some cases improving, data collection systems on child labour is an essential first step.

Raising Awareness: A common attitude toward child labour in India is to accept it as an unavoidable consequence of poverty. Given the low quality and implied costs of the education services available to the poor, many parents, having themselves worked as children, tend to consider an early entry into the labour market, rather than schooling, as the best way to equip their children with skills useful for their future as adults.

Another difficulty is inherent in the fact that children working in rural areas, in urban informal sector workshops or as domestic servants in private households are not readily visible. An effective effort to protect children from work place hazards or abuses must therefore begin by making the invisible visible. Experience clearly shows that significant public pressure is required to make progress on the child labour issue politically possible. As long as the general public, and in particular the middle and higher classes, consider that child labour is part of the harsh reality that makes good economic sense, the conditions for change will not be met.

The Government of India has restricted its role to enacting legislation, but has been passive in its enforcement. Most initiatives against child labour have traditionally come from Non-Government Organisations. In spite of their dedication however, their resources cannot be equal to the magnitude of the task. All levels of society need to do their share.

Some types of action can be provided only by the Central Government: child labour legislation and attendant enforcement mechanisms, the setting of public policy priorities and a publicly-funded system of basic education that offers quality schooling for all, including the children of the poorest families.

Trade Unions Bring Abuses to Light

Trade unions, are the logical leaders for bringing child labour abuses to light. They are ideally placed to document concrete cases of abusive child labour and to monitor the effectiveness of legal instruments and the performance of the labour inspectorate in the child labour field.

Employers and their organisations also have good reasons to be interested in the issue. Besides obvious humanitarian and social reasons, combating child labour makes perfect sense on economic and business grounds. Emotionally or physically damaged children have little chance of becoming productive adults.

NGO's Strength is With Children Already Working

Like trade unions, NGOs can help to discover and publicize specific cases of abusive child labour. They are, in addition especially good at devising and implementing action programmes on behalf of children already in the labour market. Close to the children, they generally enjoy the thrust of the local communities concerned and are well placed to appeal to their hearts and resources.

The participation of other segments of civil society—the media, universities, parliamentarians, teachers and educators—should be enlisted in the fight against child labour. All are valuable allies and can cooperate in complementary ways.

Establishing the Required Institutional Capacity

To formulate and execute a national plan of action against child labour, institutional mechanisms must be established or strengthened within the governmental apparatus. These can then be entrusted with the responsibility for setting priorities, coordinating the activities of the various ministries concerned, promoting private sector participation and for launching and supporting pilot schemes to find new ways of preventing child labour and of rehabilitating those who have been rescued from it.

Improving Legislation and Enforcement Measures

In India legislation exempts from coverage precisely the kinds of work in which children are most engaged (agriculture, family undertakings, small workshops, domestic service). A necessary first step to expanding protection under the law is to ensure that the main places where children work and the worst forms of child labour are encompassed by national legislation.

Improving Schooling for the Poor

The single most effective way to stem the flow of school-age children into abusive forms of employment or work is to extend and improve schooling so that it will attract and retain them. Recent trends however leave little room for optimism in that regard. In the eighties and early nineties resources devoted to education have dwindled steadily in India. The poor situation of the economy and the effects of structural adjustment policies were the reasons generally given for this decline.

Using Economic Incentives

As poor families need the income deriving from the employment of their children, it has often been considered appropriate to provide cash or in-kind payments as replacement.

Lively International Debate Over Negative Incentives

The advisability of using negative economic incentives has been the subject of much recent public debate. In Europe several department stores have decided not to sell products such as carpets unless they are certified to be made without child labour. Such movements by consumers and manufacturers alike have been accompanied by powerful efforts on the legislative and trade fronts as demonstrated by the hot debate on the incorporation of a social clause into international trade agreements. The United States has introduced conditionally into its Generalised System of Preferences, as has the European Union, to promote, among others, better labour standards and thereby discourage the use of child labour. A bill aiming at banning the import into the United States of goods produced by children (the Harkin Bill), has generated concern among employers and governments in countries heavily dependent on the United States for their exports.

There is no doubt that initiatives of this kind have helped significantly to raise public awareness about child labour. However, they have also had unintended consequences. The mere threat led employers of various industries to abruptly dismiss tens of thousands of children, the end result was that the dismissed children shifted to other occupations, which were often more hazardous than the jobs they used to perform in the previous industry, with no instances of children returning to school.

This example suggests that such measures may drive child labour into the less regulated domestic economic sectors. It also suggests the need to move children away from the work place in a phased and planned manner, instead of simply throwing them overnight, and unaided, into a far worse situation.

28

World Trade—The Next Challenge

On 15 December 1993 the world changed. May be not as dramatically as the moment when the Berlin Wall fell, but then unlike that very necessary demolition job, the success of the Uruguay Round was a work of construction. Like the destruction of the wall, though, its effects will be profound and lasting ones felt far beyond its immediate context. It will be seen as a defining moment in modern history.

The importance of the round can be seen in terms of boost it gives to job creation; to development; to investment; to economic reform; to the rule of law and in many other ways besides. All of these benefits are real and important. But the true value of the whole is much, more than the sum of these parts.

Put simply, governments came to the conclusion that the notion of a new world order was not merely attractive but absolutely vital; that the reality of the global market—whatever ambitions some of them may retain for regional integration—required a level of multilateral cooperation never before attempted.

No Losers in the Round

It has created a revolutionary framework for economic, legal and political cooperation. But now turn to the immediate results of the round. Seeing them as a profit and loss account or a score card of winners and losers is to see them in static terms, as one-off conclusions with finite effects. This misses the point completely.

Every nation now needs an effective trading system, but especially so the small and poor. They have it. Everyone will also gain from the huge package of market access results even if they did not get every concession they were seeking from trading partners—it is the biggest market access deal ever negotiated.

However, the essence of the Uruguay Round's achievements is that they are dynamic. The new agreements, the new rules and structures it sets up—all mean a commitment to a continuing process of cooperation and reform of which the agreement in December was only the beginning.

Maintaining the liberalising momentum will call for continuing effort and vigilance by participating countries. But now their energy can be focused through the Round's greatest innovation; the new World Trade Organisation (WTO) in place of the improvised basis on which the GATT has operated for 45 years, trade will now have a permanent forum appropriate to its importance in the world economy.

Technically, speaking, the WTO will oversee the implementation of the Round's results, administrator all the agreements in goods, services and intellectual property, and manage the unified dispute settlement system. But beyond these administrative functions, it will raise the political profile of trade a profile which has already been lifted greatly by the Uruguay Round. The WTO will have regular instead of occasional—direct Ministerial involvement. It will have a clear mandate to act as a forum for further trade negotiations. Most of all it will complete the transition from a trading system which largely restricted itself to policies at the border to one which also covers most aspects of domestic policy-making affecting international competition in goods and services, as well as investment.

Through the WTO, the Round will change the way the world economy is shaped. But it is not the final victory over protectionism and unilateralism. Any premature rejoining would have quickly been cut short by the evidence since 15 December that major economic powers are still ready to take the unilateral approach to trade problems. Arguments for protectionism based on the alleged threat of low-cost competition to production and jobs will not just fade away because the Round is a success. The seductive appeal of 'beggar-thy-neighbour' policies is highlighted by the seemingly greater vigour of the lobbies for protectionism than the advocates of open markets.

These dangers—and the speed with which they have resurfaced—make the achievement of the Uruguay Round all the more important, and its successful implementation all the more urgent. Implementation requires more than mutual backslapping about what we have achieved. It requires now that the US, EU and Japan, in particular, rapidly obtain final authority to ratify and also take a lead in providing the WTO with the means to fulfil its mandate.

The success of the Round has come at a time when it is even more vitally needed than anyone could have guessed when it was launched in 1986. Old structures and alignments have been turned inside out in trade as in every other area of international relations. We face a world of change and challenge, in which the reinforced trading system will be a primary source of stability and security.

The developing countries including India have become enthusiastic supporters of the multilateral trading system and the Uruguay Round even if all their demands were not met by industrial countries. The reasons lie in the changing economic policies of many developing countries and the clearer appreciation of the value of the GATT system that has grown along with these changes.

The challenges of new issues in world trade will be a major one for the WTO. The new organisation has to consider issues such as the links between trade and the environment, international competition policy, trade and investment, and trade and labour standards. To say a few words about trade and the environment since it is one area in which GATT member countries have committed themselves already to a comprehensive new work programme. They decided on 15 December, in conjunction with the adoption of the results of the Uruguay Round negotiations, to draw up a work programme on trade and environment by the Ministerial meeting in Marrakesh. Environmental policy-making is one of the most rapidly evolving areas of national and international policy-making, and it is entirely appropriate that emphasis should be placed now in GATT/WTO on ensuring better policy coordination and multilateral cooperation over the linkages between trade and environment.

Permanent Negotiations

The Uruguay Round may well be the last of its kind, but this in no way means the end of multilateral trade negotiations. On the contrary, it means they become a permanent event. Adhoc negotiating rounds were necessary mainly because the GATT lacked the mandate or the institutional basis to operate the multilateral system to the full on a continuous basis. Between rounds the GATT has tended to lose momentum, often at the very times when it was essential to make the most of the liberalising impulse. This has allowed protectionism and unilaterialism to recover and regroup and meant that each round has to start by regaining lost ground.

The positive results of the Uruguay Round will redefine much more than assumptions about trade. If they are exploited with the same determination, courage and commitment that went into concluding the Round, they should mean nothing less than a new start for sustainable growth and a new system of collective economic security for the world.

But if the trading system is now up to the job of supporting multilateral cooperation on such a wide scale, do the other structures of economic cooperation still meet the bill? The establishment of the WTO will put trade and investment on a par—perhaps rather in advance—of cooperation in monetary and financial areas. The WTO will stand alongside its original Bretton Woods sisters, the IMF and the World Bank. The three institutions must learn to work together even more effectively and closely. For example, rather than each body conducting separate reviews of country policies, is there not a case to be made for a more integrated approach on country reviews? But that does not, on its own, add up to effective multilateral economic cooperation. The question really has to be asked seriously: are the G7, the OECD, the regional grouping adequate to provide that cooperation?

It is the next challenge of international economic leadership—the challenge of translating the common interest in global growth into a practical and effective mechanism for solving our common economic problems together. So, the ministers meeting in Marrakesh is an historic event which will establish the World Trade Organisation and put in place the new multilateral trading system, they will be making not an end, but a beginning.

29

Rural Poverty in India

"It is morning in a remote farming area in India. As her husband harnesses a bullock to plough their field, a woman pounds the grain she will use for the day's main meal. Three kilometres away, their children are collecting fuel wood and water before starting their morning walk to school".

"After school, they help their mother light a fire with a few sticks, milk the cow and collect the sundried grain. That evening, as the family rests around the hearth, father worries about how to sell his onions before they spoil and the price falls. Before sleeping his wife prepares a basket of home-grown vegetables to sell next day at the village market five kilometres away. With the takings, she hoped to buy a kerosene lamp although she might not have enough cash left to buy the kerosene immediately. . ."

That description of rural life is a daily reality for hundreds of millions of families throughout India. Rural poverty, 1990 means subsistence on the meagre earnings of wage labour or unreliable harvests from small plots of land. It means raising a family without safe drinking water or proper sanitation, suffering disease or injury without medical assistance. In times of un-employment or crop failure, it means living with the pangs of hunger—and the risk of death by famine.

Inside the Poverty Trap

Poverty in rural India is created and perpetuated by a number of closely interlinked socio-economic processes:

1. Policies and institutional arrangements biased against the poor exclude them from the benefits of development, frustrate their productive potential and accentuate the impact of other poverty processes.

   Institutional processes that perpetuate rural poverty include lack of access to land, inequitable share-cropping and tenancy arrangements, poor markets, limited access to credit, inputs and technology, and ineffective extension services. Other constraints are lack of training facilities, inadequate research related to small-holder farming systems, and last but not least a lack of grass-roots institutions needed to foster people's participation.

   Policy and institutional biases have short and long-term impacts. In the short term, the poor are unable to earn enough to meet nutritional requirements or to take advantage of the market. 'In the longer term', "poor households continue to lag behind because they do not generate a surplus for investment, nor do they have access to investment opportunities. Moreover, the rural poor may be forced to overuse resources, which undermines productivity and income".

2. Even today dualistic agrarian structures originating in colonial times persist. In India,

highly capitalised large and medium-sized farms have virtually monopolistic control over land and labour at the expense of the small farm sector. Large scale commercial producers—control the best farm land. Resources have been funneled into irrigated plantations producing cotton and mechanised cultivation of sorghum. In marginal areas, mechanisation has led to environmental degradation and the loss of seasonal grazing and stork routes for pastoralists.

"Thus, side by side with modern agriculture, millions of marginal farmers and herdsmen subsist far below the poverty line". This dualism severely limits their capacity to grow food and accumulate capital. They lack marketable surpluses, and incentives and opportunities to save and invest.

3. Rapid population growth can cause and perpetuate rural poverty by increasing pressure on limited productive resources, social services and employment, as well as—paradoxically—creating labour shortage through outmigration.

   The most obvious consequence of rapid population growth is that, even with relatively high rates of economic growth, improvements in living conditions are limited. Total saving in the economy declines, leaving fewer resources for investment in human development. Negative consequences are most acute in rural areas. Growing population often combined with traditional laws of inheritance—has led to fragmentation of holdings, degradation of crop and pasture land, and falling yields. In areas with unequal distribution of land, rapid population growth has accelerated proletarisation of the rural work force and reduced incomes.

4. Rural poverty malnutrition and undernutrition are closely linked to environmental degradation. Poor people in marginal areas are destroying natural resources as they struggle to keep their production systems sustainable. In acute shortage of arable land has forced farmers to reduce the length of fallow periods and plough up land previously reserved for grazing. These practices have led to declining yields, soil depletion and further impoverishment. Population pressure is pushing weaker members of the rural community into ecologically vulnerable areas.

   Degradation of the environment is strongly linked to household food insecurity and lack of fuel. Much of the fragile forest cover has been destroyed by poor rural people in the search for grazing land and fuel wood.

   Government policies have also wrought environmental damage. A rapid expansion of areas under crops often accelerates deforestation and land degradation. Programmes to expand cereal production into marginal areas, subsidised capital to support commercial operations subsidies for inappropriate technologies and excessive transfer of income out of the agricultural sector may undermine the sustainability of small holders and pastoralists' production systems.

   Inadequate public investment in off-farm employment and infrastructure, a lack of price incentives and inadequate access to modern agricultural inputs and services discourage investment in land conservation, leading to further overuse and degradation.

5. As poverty undermines traditional social bonds, the marginalisation of women has become a fact

of rural life in India. With little or no access to land, millions of women depend on casual employment on meagre wages. Often, they farm fragmented plots of poor quality. Limited access to inputs, extension, training and credit limits, in turn, their ability to enter commercial agriculture.

The exodus of males in search of work in urban areas (itself an indicator of poverty) has serious consequences for the women they leave behind. Output from land often falls and less attention is paid to maintenance, setting the stage for a long-term decline in productivity. Many female headed households have abandoned the use of oxen for ploughing, some plough and plant late and others no longer weed their fields.

6. The ethnic or cultural marginalisation of tribal or minority populations also plays a role in poverty. Many of these groups are further threatened by newly marginalised groups—as the expansion of cultivation reduces the grazing areas of nomadic herders.

7. Exploitative middlemen also perpetuate rural poverty. Landlords exploit share croppers and tenants, moneylenders exploit debtors, and traders exploit small scale producers. During seasonal food shortages, the poor may have to borrow money at interest rates exceeding 20 per cent a month. Forced to devote most of their energies to debt servicing, they sink deeper into the poverty trap.

In some cases, government controlled cooperatives and government agencies whose task is to protect the poor may themselves practise forms of exploitation. Heavy levies imposed by government agencies have damaged small farmers. Large, inefficient bureaucracies are paid for buy the productive sectors of the community and frequently contribute to the accumulation of large budget deficits.

8. Political troubles and civil strife have had a disastrous impact on the rural poor one effect is the disruption of development assistance to the rural poor, both from national and international agencies. Another is the transformation of many producers into consumers of social services with serious consequences for production, savings, capital accumulation and investment.

9. The international economic environment directly influences the well-being of the Indian poor. Falling commodity prices and protectionist policies in India affect the employment and incomes of plantation workers and small-holders producing for export, particularly those relying heavily on a few agricultural commodities. Changes in international interest rates have repeatedly hurt small-scale producers in debt-burdened India, while world grain price increases has triggered rural famines.

The net flow of development resources to agriculture also affects rural poverty. Official development funding for food and agriculture increased between 1975 and 1982, but has fluctuated irregularly since. Moreover, concern with trade balances is diverting resources to export crops, sometimes at the expense of traditional crops grown by poor farmers.

30

Technological Entrepreneurship: The New Force for Economic Growth

Entrepreneurship has emerged as a major force for change. The dynamic role of modern small business in economic growth has received fresh recognition worldwide. It is essential to promote entrepreneurship and to mobilise the dynamism of the private sector for accelerated national development. An unbridled private sector may not, however, ensure growth with equity. It is the prime responsibility of governments to create policy frameworks that enable businesses to apply technology for competitive advantage and for the well-being of the public.

The Changing Global Environment

As agents of change and progress, entrepreneurs start by identifying a market opportunity and matching this with social or technical innovations. They then proceed to mobilise the resources necessary to drive their business concept to its commercial realisation. The development of a product or service with a high-technology content—never easy anywhere, or at today's rapidly-changing global environment. It calls for restructuring the available technology and business development systems and developing the skills needed by a new breed of 'techno-entrepreneurs' to transform innovations into market opportunities at home and abroad. It also requires reorienting the present processes and priorities of technical and economic cooperation among countries.

Amidst the global concerns of environmental preservation, poverty elimination and social development, the practical problems of entrepreneurship are not being properly addressed, even though entrepreneurs will create the bulk of enterprises, jobs and wealth.

A torrent of technology-based goods hits the market every week, ostensibly improving the quality of our lives while simultaneously creating complexity and dislocation. The pace of progress in information, technologies, microelectronics, robotics, new materials, biomedical sciences, space science and other advanced technologies quickens, significantly changing the way we live. The growth of markets for these technologies also proceeds apace.

Further, technological change is taking place today against a background of growing intra-national and international disequilibria. While the transformation from State-centred to market-oriented development is opening up enormous opportunities and options, it has also caused severe short-term hardships. In order to survive and prosper in these changing times, India and its enterprises need enlightened government policies, good technical infrastructure and strong cultural roots.

Traditional production factors are giving way to a new paradigm characterised by new patterns of trade, investment and employment, and by informal networking life-long learning and technological entrepreneurship. The manufacturing sector in India continues to be dominated by food products, textiles, chemicals and other traditional industry, mainly in the public sector. However, change is coming, albeit slowly. State enterprises are being corporatised pending privatisation, and the share of knowledge-based and information-related activities in the marketplace is rising perceptibly. Restructuring policies now place emphasis (often purely rhetorical) on the role of the private sector. The legacy of decades of centrally-planned development is generally inimical to private enterprise. In turn, the private sector has been slow to respond to economic liberalisation in India and generally failed to generate the new employment necessary to absorb new entrants to the labour force.

The regulatory problems of an onerous tax structure and administration, poor access to finance and raw materials, over-regulation of labour and land use, pervasive bureaucracy and restricted markets have been significant barriers to entrepreneurial growth.

Towards Competitive Performance

The imperative of improved performance has serious implications for India if it is to survive, stay abreast and succeed. It calls for national efforts on systemic efficiency and productivity growth, the move from an investment-driven to an innovation-driven economy and sustained higher-order competitiveness; towards enhanced customer satisfaction at home and penetration of selected markets abroad. Concurrently, governments and business have to address such intractable problems as poverty, corruption and the degradation of the environment.

Creating New Technology-Based Ventures

Starting a new business in India is a hazardous task. Problems are compounded when the venture is technology-based:

- Capital requirements are generally larger, while traditional banks are ill-equipped to process the perceived risk. Venture capital generally only becomes an option when the venture has documented the merits of its management, market and innovation.
- Knowledge-based ventures can benefit from linkages to sources of knowledge—*e.g.* the technical university or research lab. Such mentoring needs to be cultivated.
- Techno-entrepreneurs often have technical skills but usually lack the business management and marketing skills necessary for success. These need to be supplemented.
- In fields where technology is changing rapidly, it is often advantageous to make technology-acquisition arrangements. Sourcing such innovations, negotiating technology licensing agreements and protecting the intellectual property itself require special skills.
- Knowledge-based innovations are inherently more risky than others. The management of this unique risk requires assessment techniques and vision.
- Technology-based ventures often have social and environmental implications, which need to be managed carefully.
- Penetrating a competitive market requires good market intelligence, a good strategic plan and good luck.

Special Characteristics of 'Techno-Entrepreneurs'

The popular misconceptions are that techno-entrepreneurs are born, not made; that they take risks with other people's money and fail more often than they succeeded. In fact, entrepreneur skills can be identified and developed. The entrepreneur is typically an innovator who formulates new solutions to existing problems, mobilises resources and stimulates others to participate in his or her team. These aptitudes develop over time, often starting in childhood, as the person faces new challenges and learns from failure.

Entrepreneurial opportunities can be found in every industrialising country, community and family. Principal sources of entrepreneurs for knowledge-based ventures are often the university and government research laboratories, the large industrial and military establishments and professional service firms. Some motivations of the entrepreneur are the need to: be independent; creative value; contribute to society; earn recognition; become rich or; quite often, simply not to be unemployed. Value-adding ventures with good growth potential can best be developed in an open market and in a culture which supports risk-taking.

The techno-entrepreneur anywhere has the challenge of moving a concept through the prototype and production phase towards creation of a product which meets market needs at a price consistent with the value created and with the ability of customers to pay.

Equally, important, the market itself has to be developed and sustained. It is not enough to be first with a better mousetrap if one does not have the skills to educate and reach potential buyers and to set the market standard.

Hence one has to distinguish between innovators and inventors. The inventor is typically a creative person in a quest for knowledge or for producing new products, without determining in advance whether a real market exists for his or her inventions. On the other hand, the innovator draws on existing knowledge and the talents of others to develop or adapt a product or service at a volume and cost that can capture a significant portion of an identified market. The flexibility and creativity of a small entrepreneurial techno-venture may lead to more incremental and breakthrough innovations than can be generated by larger-sized firms in many sectors.

The pace and pattern of India's economic development now depend in large measure on its technical resource base. In this context, the key determinants are the skills to apply technology for enhanced competitiveness, as well as to create teachbased ventures. Techno-entrepreneurs have to be supported by appropriate national structures and international linkages if they are to survive and flourish in an intensely competitive world.

Bibliography

Ackoff, R.L., *Redesigning the Future: A Systems Approach to Societal Problems* (John Wiley, 1974).

Adelman, I., et. al. *Economic Growth and Social Equality in Developing Countries* (California, Standford University, 1967).

Aggarwal, Y.P., *Education and Human Resource Development* (New Delhi, Commonwealth, 1988).

Amirk Singh., New Policy on Education: Two Years Later', *Economic and Political Weekly*, Special Number, Vol. XXIII. Nos. 45, 46, and 47, pp. 2479-92.

Anand, Mulk Raj, 'A Nation of Illiterates' *The Tribune*. Feb. 12, 1991.

Anderson, C.A., 'A Skeptical Note on Education and Mobility', A.H. Halsey, and Others (ed)—*Education Economy and Society*, (New York, The Free Press, 1969), pp. 164-182.

Anderson, C.A., 'Access to Higher Education and Economic Development' in *Halsey, A.H. (Ed)-op. cit.* Work. pp. 252-268.

Anderson, C.A. and Bowman, M.J., *Education and Economic Development* (Chicago; 1965).

Anon, 'The Pressure of Economic Change' in A.H. Halsey, (Ed), *op. cit.* pp. 22-30.

Anon, 'All-out Bid to Tap Human Resources', *The Economic Times* (Supplement), Dec. 20, 1984, pp. 1-3.

Asharaya, P., 'Education: Politics and Social Structure' *Economic and Political Weekly*, Vol. XX, No. 42, Oct. 19, 1985, pp. 1785-89.

Bantock, G.A. *Education and Values,* (London, Faber and Faber, 1966).

Bauer, R.A. (Ed), *Social Indicators* (Cambridge and London, MIT Press, 1966).

Becker, Garry S., *Human Capital* (Princeton, Princeton University Press, 1964).

Becker, Garry S., *Human Capital: A Theoretical and Empirical Analysis with Special Reference to Education*, (New York, NBER, 1974).

Ben-Porath, Yoram. 'The Production of Human Capital and the Life Cycle of Earnings', *The Journal of Political Economy*, August, 1967, pp. 352-65.

Benson, Charles S. *Perspectives on the Economics of Education* (Boston, Houghton Mifflin Company, 1963).

Bhalla, G.S. and Bhalla, H.S. 'Human Resource Development for Rural Poor', Paper presented at the *U.G.C. National Seminar*, held at G.K.I.A.S. in Rural Development, Punjabi University, Campus, Damdama Sahib).

Bhatia, S.K., 'Challenges in Human Resource Management', *Indian Management*, Vol. 25, No. 8, August 1986, pp. 5-12.

Blaug, Mark (Ed), *Economics of Education-I* (New York, Penguin, 1968).

Blaug, Mark (Ed), *Economics of Education-II* (New York, Penguin, 1969).

Blaug, Mark, *An Introduction to the Economics of Education* (New York, Penguin, 1970).

Blaug, Mark, 'The Empirical Status of Human Capital Theory: Slightly Jaundiced Survey', *Journal of Economic Literature*, Vol. 14, No. 3, September 1976, pp. 827-55.

Boulding, K., *The Meaning of the Twentieth Century* (London, Allen and Unwin, 1965).

Bowman, M.J., 'Education and Economic Growth *in King, I. (Ed), Education and Income* (Staff Working Paper No. 402, Washington, World Bank, 1980) pp. 1-71.

Bowman, M.J., 'The Human Investment Revolution in Economic Thought', *Sociology of Education* 39/2 (Spring), pp. 111-37.

Brown, Murraya (Ed), *The Theory and Empirical Analysis of Production* (New York, NBER, 1967).

Brownstein, L., *Education and Development in Rural Kenya* (New York, Praeger, 1972).

Burgess, T., et. al., *Manpower and Educational Development in India* (London, Oliver and Boynd).

Byars, L.L. and Rue, L.W., *Human Resource Management* (Illinois, Irwin Homewood).

Chattopadhyay, G., 'Education: The Authority to Learn or the Authority of the Bowl of Hemlock' in *Decision* (IIM, Calcutta), Vol. 16, No. 1, Jan-March, 1989, pp. 22-33.

Cheema, C.S. 'The Challenges of Human Resource Development in Rural Punjab'—Paper Presented at *U.G.C. National Seminar* held at G.K.I.A.S. in Rural Development, Punjabi University Campus, Damdama Sahib).

Clark, Harold F., *'The Return on Educational Investment' in C.S. Benson,* (Ed), *op. cit.*, 1963, pp. 24-32.

Coombs, P.H. and Manzoor Ahmed, *Attacking Rural Poverty: Non-Formal Education Can Help* (John Hopkins University Press, 1974).

Coombs, P.H., *The World Crisis in Education: The View from Eighties* (Oxford, OUP, 1985).

Correa, Hector, *The Economics of Human Resources* (Amsterdam, North-Holland, 1963).

Curle, Adam, 'Some Aspects of Educational Planning in Underdeveloped Areas, *Harvard Educational Review*, Vol. 32, No. 3, 1962.

D'Souza, A.A. and De Souza., A. *Population Growth and Human Development* (Delhi, ISI, 1974).

Datta, S., 'Human Resource Development', *Man and Development*, Vol. 8, No. 1, March 1986, pp. 9-17.

Davis, R.G., *Planning Human Resource Development,* (Chicago, 1966).

Davis, Russel G. *Planning Human Resource Development: Education Models and Schemata* (Chicago, CSED, Harvard University, 1966).

Denison, Edward F., 'Education and Growth' in Benson, C.S. (Ed), *op. cit.,* pp. 33-42.

Desai A.R. *Social Background of Indian Nationalism* (Bombay, Popular, 1966).

Deshmukh, C.D. 'Management and Administration: New Trends', *Training Abstracts 17,* New Delhi Training Division, 1972.

Dey, B., 'On Costing Education' in Pandit's *Measurement of Cost Productivity and Efficiency of Education* (New Delhi, NCERT, 1969), pp. 14-26.

Dey, B., 'Training in the Civil Services: Plea for A Holistic Construal', *Indian Journal of Public Administration* Vol. XXIV, No. 4, Oct.-Dec. 1982.

Drucker, Peter F. 'The Educational Revolution' in Halsey and Others (Ed) *op. cit.,* pp. 15-21.

Drucker, Peter, F., *Managing in Turbulent Times* (William Heinemann, 1980).

Dwivedi, R.S., *Management of Human Resources: A Behavioural Approach to Personnel* (New Delhi, Oxford and IBH, 1982).

Farooq, Khan A., 'Development of Human Resources', *The Economic Times*, September 22, 1984.

Gandhi, Rajiv, 'New National Policy on Education', *Inaugural Address* at the Conference of Education Ministers at New Delhi, August 29, 1985.

Gill, K.S., 'Agricultural Development in Punjab' in Johar and Khanna's (Ed), *Studies in Punjab Economy* (Amritsar, GNDU, 1983).

Gore, M.S., 'Literacy: Equaliser of Opportunity', *Democratic World*, March 31, 1991, Vol. XX. No. 13.

Gostkowski, Z. *Towards A System of Human Resources Indicators for Less-Developed Countries* (The Polish Academy of Sciences).

Government of India, *Challenges of Education: A Policy Perspective* (Government of India, Ministry of Education, 1985).

Government of India, *National Policy on Education* (New Delhi, Govt. of India, 1986).

Government of India, *National Policy on Education: Programme of Action* (New Delhi, Govt. of India, 1986).

Groves, Harold M., 'Education and Economic Growth' in C.S. Benson, (Ed), *op. cit.*, pp. 7-11.

Halsey, A.H. and Others (Ed), *Education, Economy and Society* (New York, the Free Press, 1969).

Harbison, F., 'The Prime Movers of Innovations' in Halsey, A.H. and Others (Ed) *op. cit.*

Harbison, F. *Human Resources as the Wealth of Nations* (London, OUP, 1973).

Harbison, F. and Myers, C.A. *Education, Manpower and Economic Growth* (New York, 1974).

Havighurst, R.J., 'Education and Social Mobility' in Four Societies' in A.H. Halsey, and Others (Ed), *op. cit.*, pp. 105-120.

Heyneman, S.P., *Improving the Quality of Education in Developing Countries* (Washington, World Bank, 1983).

Heyneman, S.P. and White, D.S., *The Quality of Education and Economic Development* (Washington, World Bank, 1986).

Hicks, Norman, *Economic Growth and Human Resources*, World Bank, Staff Paper No. 408, (Washington, World Bank, 1980).

Hilton School of *Human Resource Development* (Vellore, ISSR, 1989).

Huq, M.S., *Education, Manpower and Development in South and South-East Asia* (Delhi, Sterling, 1975).

Hussain, Majid, *Agricultural Geography* (New Delhi, Inter-India, 1986).

Jagannathan, N., 'Gender Equality in Education', *University News*, Vol. XXIX, No. 5, Feb. 4, 1991, pp. 1-5.

Jamison, D.T. and Laurence, J.L., *Farmer Education and Farm Efficiency* (Baltimore, John Hopkins, 1982).

Jhingan, M.L., *The Economics of Development and Planning* (New Delhi, Vikas, 1975).

Johnson, D. Gale., 'Economics and the Educational System, in C.S. Benson, (Ed), *op. cit.*, pp. 374-80.

Joshi, P.C., 'Role of Culture in Social Transformation and National Integration, *Economic and Political Weekly*, Vol. XXI, No. 28.

Kamat, A.R., *Progress of Education in Rural Maharashtra* (Pune, Gokhale Institute of Politics and Economics, 1968).

Khanna, G., Parkash, S. and Bansal, R.K., *Unit Cost of College Education in Punjab* (Patiala, Punjabi University, 1985) Mimeo.

Khullar, K.K., 'Four Decades of Education', *Yojana*, Vol. 33, No. 8, Nov. 1-15, 1989, pp. 12-4.

King, T. (Ed)., *Education and Income*, World Bank Staff Working, Paper No. 402, (Washington, World Bank, 1980).

Kirpal, P. 'How To Plan Education of The Future', *Yojana*, Vol. 33, No. 14 and 15, August, 1989.

Kothari, Commission, *Report of the Education Commission: 1964-66* (Delhi, Government of India, 1970).

Kothari, V.N. and Panchamukhi, P.R., 'Economics of Education: A Trend Report' in *ICSSR's A Survey of Research in Economics* (New Delhi, 1980), pp. 169-238.

Krishnamurthy, H.V. 'Human Resource Development Strategy For 21st Century; *P.U. Management Review*, Vol. 9, Nos. 1 and 2, Jan-Feb. 1986, pp. 79-89.

Kulkarni, V.G. 'Alternatives in Education' *Man and Development* (Vol. VIII), March 1985, pp. 25-58.

Lipton, *Why Poor Stay Poor: A Study of Urban Bias in World Development* (London, Templesmith, 1977).

MacNamara, R.S. *The Assault on World Poverty* (Washington, World Bank, 1975).

Mahajan, V.S. 'Whither National Policy: Education', *The Tribune,* Feb. 24, 1991, p. 8.

Majumdar, Tapas. *Investment in Education and Social Choice,* (New York, Cambridge University Press, 1983).

Marshall, Alfred. 'Education and Invention' in Benson, C.S. (Ed), *op. cit.*, pp. 82-83.

Mathur, B.L. (Ed)., *Human Resource Development: Strategic Approaches and Experiences,* (Jaipur, Arihant, 1989).

Mathur, R.N., *Population Analysis and Studies* (Allahabad, Chugh).

Megginson, L.C., *Personnel and Human Resource Administration,* 1974.

Mehta, M.M., *Human Resource Development Planning,* (Delhi, Macmillan, 1976).

Mingat, Alan and Tan, Jee-Pang. *Analytical Tools for Sector Work in Education* (Baltimore/London, John Hopkins University Press, 1988).

Mishra, L. 'Literacy: Now or Never' in *Yojana*, Vol. 34, No. 20, Nov. 1-15, 1990, pp. 4-5.

Misra, S.K. and Puri, V.K., *Development and Planning: Theory and Practice,* (Bombay, Himalaya, 1986).

Moddie, A.D. *Explorations in Management Development* (New Delhi, AIMA, 1976).

Myrdal, G., *Asian Drama* (Penguin, 1963).

Nadler, L., *Developing Human Resources* (Texas, Concepts, 1979).

Nadler, L., *The Handbook of Human Resources Development* (John Willey, 1984).

Nallagounden, A.M. 'Investment in Education in India' *Journal of Human Resource,* Vol. 2, No. 3, Summer-1967, pp. 347-58.

Nandedkar, V.G., 'Human Resource: Both an End and Means' *Yojana*, Vol. 34, Nos. 1 and 2, Jan. 26, 1990, pp. 50-53.

National Council of Educational Research and Training. *The Fourth All India Education Survey* (New Delhi, NCERT, 1982).

Niland, John R., *The Production of Manpower Specialists: A Volume of Selected Papers* (New York, Cornell, University, 1971).

Nurkse, R., *Problems of Capital Formation in Underdeveloped Countries*, (New Delhi, OUP, 1973).

OECD, *Education in OECD Developing Countries: Trends and Perspectives,* (France, OECD, 1974).

Ota, Masao. 'Quantitative Method For the Planning of Human Resource Development', *Research Bulletin of the National Institute for Educational Research*, No. 11, 1972, pp. 25-41.

Panchamukhi, V.R. Leading Issues in Human Resource Development in India' in P.R. Brahmananda, and V.R. Panchamukhi, (Ed), *Development Process of the Indian Economy,* (Bombay, Himalaya, 1987), pp. 1060-1108.

Pandit, H.N., *Measurement of Cost Productivity and Efficiency of Education* (Delhi, NCERT, 1969).

Pandit, H.N., A Study of Unit Costs at School Stage in India: A Design of the Research Project (Pandit, H.N. (Ed), *1969, op. cit.,* pp. 3-13.

Panigrahi, D. 'Human Resource Development in Business Administration', B.L. Mathur, (Ed), *op. cit.*

Parkash, Shri., *Educational System of India: An Econometric Study* (Delhi, Concept, 1978).

Parminder Kaur, and Singh, Bhawdeep,. 'Human Resource Development in Rural Punjab' in *U.G.C. National Seminar* held at G.K.I.A.S. in Rural Development (Punjabi University Campus), Damdama Sahib, 22-23 Feb., 1991.

Patel, S.J., 'Educational Miracle in The Third World', *Economic and Political Weekly,* Vol. XX, No. 31, August 3, 1985, pp. 1312-17.

Patil, V.T. and Patil, B.C., *Problems in Indian Education* (New Delhi, Oxford and IBH, 1982).

Perlman, R., *The Economics of Education: Conceptual Problems and Policy Issues* (McGraw Hill, 1973).

Paillai, S.S., 'Educational System and Social Structure', *Educational India,* Vol. 9, March, 1973.

Planning Commission., *The Sixth Five Year Plan: 1980-85* (New Delhi, Government of India).

Planning Commission., *The First Five Plan: 1951-56* (Delhi, Government of India).

Psachorapoulos, G., *Earnings and Education in OECD Countries* (Paris, OECD, 1973).

Psachorapoulos, G., 'Education and Development—A Review', *Pigmy Economic Review,* Monthly Economic Journal of the Syndicate Bank, Oct. 88, Vol. 34, No. 3.

Punit, A.E., *Social System in Rural India* (New Delhi, Sterling, 1978).

Radakrishnan, S., *The Creative Life.*

Index

Adult Education, 49-50

African charter on Human and People's Right, 83

AIDS, 88, 91-94

  Change in sexual practice, 92

  Estimates of, 91

  Information on developing as disease, 93

  Media and, 92-93

  Obstacles to launch publicity campaigns, 93-94

  Spreading in Africa and Asia, 92-93

American Convention on Human Rights, 83

Apollo Groups, 39

Asia-Pacific Economic Cooperation, 4

Bangladesh, 59

Brazil, 16

Broader approach to education, 47-50

  Adult education, 49-50

  Building bridges between cultures, 47-49

  Literacy, 47-48

Cardiovascular disease, 98

Child labour, 109-15

  Action required at national level, 111

  Child slaves, 111

  Establishing required institutional capacity, 114

  Factors affecting supply of, 110

  Girls tend to work longer hours than do boys, 109-10

  Improving legislation and enforcement measures, 114

  Improving schooling for the poor, 114

  International debate over negative incentives, 115

  More boys than girls works, 109

  NGO's strength is children already working, 113

  No effective programmes without hard information, 112-13

  Population of working children, 109

  Prostitution, 110

  Threats to health and safety, 110

  Trade unions bring abuses to light, 113

Children's health and the environment, 71-73

  Children's vulnerability, 71-72

  Environmental hazards, 71

  International awareness, 73

  Potential for prevention, 72-73

  Public health threats, 72

Child slaves, 111

Chile, 29

Convention on elimination of all forms of discrimination against women, 83
Convention on the Rights of the Child, 83
Corporate ambitions in education on, 11-14
Corporate model of reforms, 13-14
Reforming local schools, 12
Schools become levers to attract business investment, 11-14
To restore equilibrium of goals, 14

Declaration of Human Rights, 83

Federation of Private Schools, 7
Fortune 500 companies, 39
Framework convention on Tobacco control, 96
France, 5

General Agreement on Trade in Service, 1-2
Global Agreement on Tariffs and Trade, 96

Harkin Bill, 115
Health care relief in conflict situation, 102-08
Coping strategies in African Trouble zones, 106-07
Donor's perceptions in designing relief interventions, 104-05
Food relief experience, 102
Food relief for health sector, 107-08
Food relief in conflict situations, 106
Impact of conflict on health care, 102-03
Responding to local needs, 105-06
Helping your child learn, 17-18
Higher education, 23-28
Funds shortage crisis, 23-24
Missing link between education and world of work, 24-28
Unemployment graduate, 23

International finance Corp., 7

Lesotho, 58
London School of Hygiene and Tropical medicine, 96

National Institute for Information Technology, 9-10
Netherlands, 16
New Zealand, 2
Non communicable disease, 98-101
Cardio vascular disease, 98-99
Health problems for adult, 99
Leading cause of death, 98
Planning and Co-ordination, 101
Preventable, 99-101
Rise in developing countries, 99
Risk factor intervention, 100

OECD, 25, 29

Phoenix university, 39
Policy researchers and policy, 51-55
Demand side challenges, 51-52
Impact down the road, 53-54
Supply side challenge of academic research, 52-53
What to do, 54-55
Population growth and education, 56-58
Budget stress on govt., 57-58
Growth in Africa, 57
Renewed commitment to education, 57
School age population, 56-57

Private Education, 6-10
  Flourishing, 6
  How govt. schools serve the poor, 6
  Loosen regulations and set up voucher schemes, 7-10
Promotion of higher education in research, 19-22
  Measures at efficiency of system in, 20-21
  New areas of, 22
  Prospects, 22
  Science based and technology driven higher education institution, 19-20
  University role in, 19
Public Report on Basic Education in India, 6-7, 9

Rural poverty in India, 121-26
  Inside poverty trap, 122-26
  Rural life, 121-22

Safe motherhood Action for, 79-82
  Legislative and policy actions, 79-82
    Abortion, 82
    Adolescents and children, 80-81
    Barriers to access, 81
    Delegation of authority, 82
    Family planning, 80
    Regulation of practice, 81-82
Safe motherhood is a human right issue, 83-85
  Death during pregnancy, 83
  Govt. action to, 85
  Human rights relevance, 83-84
    Rights relating to equality and nondiscrimination, 84
    Rights relating to foundation of families and family life, 84
    Rights relating to health care, 84
    Rights relating to life, liberty and security of person, 83-84
Sahara, 57
Secondary and primary education, 3
Shaking ivory tower, 29-36
  Completion rates in upper secondary education, 30
  Democratisation and economic competitiveness on higher education, 32-33
  Democratisation and higher education, 31
  Democratisation and knowledge society, 35
  Enrolment rate in higher education, 29-30
  Higher education changing nature of labour market, 31
  Prospects for next half century, 33-34
  Skill requirement, 31-32
  University have changed radically, 29
South Korea, 4
Sudden Infant Death Syndrome, 72

Technological entrepreneurship, 127-32
  Changing global environment, 127-29
  Characteristics of, 130-32
  Competitive performance, 129
  Creating new technology based ventures, 129-30
Thailand, 96
Tigray, 105
Tobacco epidemic, 95-97
  Control efforts, 95-97
  Smoke death, 95
  Tobacco related disease, 95

Towards healthy cities, 66-70
City authorities, 69
city life, 67
Disease burden, 66
Ecologically unsustainable, 67
High densities allow lower costs for supply of water, 66-67
Housing loan, 68
Poor quality of housing, 66
Sanitation and drainage, 67
Supporting change, 67-70
Tuberculosis, 88-90
Case of public health crisis, 90
Characteristics of, 89
Inert TB infections, 89
Number of cases, 90
Resurgence of, 88
Stigma attached to, 89
To identify and diagnose, 90

Unemployment problem, 62-65
Agriculture, 64-65
Change of work, 63
De-jobbing, 63
Generate employment, 64
Job, 62-63
Job shift, 64
Knowledge worker, 63
Part time work, 64
UNESCO, 58
Uruguay round, 116-19
US, 3-4, 24

Violence in schools, 15-16
Passing the torch, 16
Tackling segregation, 15-16

WHO, 73, 96
WHO Non-communicative disease and mental health surveillance, 101
Will education go to market, 1-5
Education for export, 3-4
Fighting for market share, 4-5
Pressures for change, 2-3
Public spending on education, 2
Wiring up the Ivory Towers, 37-41
E-learning courses, 38
E-learning market, 37
Faculty view of e-learning, 40-41
Govt. funding decreased, 37
Information technology training courses, 39
MBA dominate e-learning, 39-40
On line learning, 38-39
Women, 59-61
Equality in society, 59-61
Improving access to education, 59-60
Secular feminist movements, 60-61
Victims, 59
Women's status, 60
World education market, 37
World trade, 116-20
No losers in Uruguay round, 117-19
Permanent negotiations, 119-20
World Trade Organisation, 1-4, 117-19

Zimbabwe, 96